Cabin

KITCHENS & BATHS

Cabin

KITCHENS & BATHS

Written and photographed by

FRANKLIN AND ESTHER SCHMIDT

GIBBS SMITH, PUBLISHER

SALT LAKE CITY

Dedicated to Bernard and Marion Godwin and Joseph and Emma Schmidt, without whom this book—and its authors—would not have been possible. And to Jigmop at Dogpatch.

FIRST EDITION

08 07 06 05 04   5 4 3 2 1

Text and photographs © 2004 Franklin and Esther Schmidt

PUBLISHED BY

Gibbs Smith, Publisher

P.O. Box 667

Layton, Utah 84041

Orders: (1-800) 748-5439
www.gibbs-smith.com

DESIGN AND COMPOSITION BY

Steve Rachwal

Printed and bound in Hong Kong

Library of Congress Cataloging-in-Publication Data

Schmidt, Franklin.
Cabin kitchens & baths / written and photographed by Franklin and
Esther Schmidt.—1st ed.
p. cm.
ISBN 1-58685-301-5
1. Kitchens. 2. Bathrooms. 3. Log cabins. 4. Interior decoration.
I. Title: Cabin kitchens and baths. II. Schmidt, Esther. III.
Title.
NK2117.K5 S35 2004
728.7'3—dc22
2003025035

ACKNOWLEDGEMENTS

We thank our editors at the superb log and timber-frame magazines who have supported us in our creative expression: A special thanks to Roland Sweet, editor-in-chief, *Log Homes Illustrated* and *Timber Homes Illustrated,* who introduced us to the log industry; Kevin Ireland, editor-in-chief, *Log Home Living;* Tracy Ruff, editor, *Timber Frame Homes;* Teresa Hilgenberg, editor, *Log Home Design Ideas;* Diane Hintz, publisher, Brooke C. Stoddard, editor, Laura Cleveland, managing editor, *Country's Best Log Homes;* also all our other editors and art directors at many of the other magazines for which we work on so many exciting and challenging projects.

We appreciate our relationships with the log and timber-frame manufacturers whose beautiful products appear in these pages; they continue to impress us with the quality of their workmanship. We are genuinely touched by the graciousness and hospitality shown us by the hundreds of homeowners throughout North America. They have welcomed us and our cameras into their homes; many have introduced us to their dogs and cats and the occasional horse, who have also become friends.

Thanks also to the contributors to this book who generously spent their time and efforts sharing their professional expertise with us and our readers. Their input vastly adds to the quality of this book.

We thank: Jeff Urbanski, who is godfather and caring camp counselor to our motley crew when we're away from home doing our thing; Erika Gardener, who is guardian at Dogpatch and reliably cares for our home and family, keeping them safe and secure while we're on the road; and James and Ricky Shaw, who ensure that our trips are safe and that our vehicles stop running only when we want them to; Mike Langford and team at Capital Color, whose professionalism and sense of perfection with our film is always exacting; Bill Moretz at Pro Camera, whose standards of camera repair and maintenance are at the pinnacle of his profession.

A few of many great friends who we wish to acknowledge are Bob and Maureen Norton Hawk; Fr. Peter Jacobs; Issac Abramson, mentor to many; Bob Cox, the best teacher ever; Kevin Appel, our friend and guide; Pete Cecere, our *consigliere* and consistently supportive Sicilian brother; KaSal and P.W., who've always been there.

We wish to acknowledge the support of our friends and neighbors in our adopted home, Rappahannock County, Virginia, who have become our extended family. (They know who they are.)

Not to be omitted—or else—our families: Dito, Beth, Bernie and August on the West Coast, and Michael and Carmen in the East. Through the years we traveled together with them over rocky and clear roads, rumble strips and speed bumps, through toll booths, tunnels, expressways and on horseback—most roads far better than worse.

Special acknowledgement and thanks to Suzanne Taylor, editorial director at Gibbs Smith, Publisher, whose experience and support guided us through the circuitous route of this project that at first seemed easy, then impossible, then doable and finally—finally—is finished.

—F & E

CONTENTS

Introduction

CABIN FEVER
is
CONTAGIOUS

Everyone dreams of a getaway cabin—a place of rest and refuge. Common usage defines *cabin* as a small, rough building made of wood. Webster likens it to a cottage, and this is defined as a small, one-story vacation house. Both definitions have come a long way. In today's design vernacular, cottage and cabin are less about roughing it and more about informal, relaxing spaces where we spend time away from our formal lives. Cabins have also evolved to full-time homes where people live year-round in their "home away from home."

The word *log* is often associated with cabin—and for good reason. In fact, log cabins have never been more popular. Hundreds of companies are manufacturing new log homes. This market is huge and growing. People are also buying up old log cabins and restoring them. Some cabins aren't log at all, but simple wood structures, including stick-built and post and beam, with both wood and Sheetrock walls. Today's log home is also no longer just a simple 400-square-foot building with one or two rooms. Usually rustic and informal in design, it can actually encompass thousands of square feet

A barrel of fun! Inexpensive and simple design details create this unique farm-themed bathroom.

containing luxurious, upscale bathrooms that contemporary homeowners have come to expect and expansive kitchens that incorporate all the bells and whistles of a sophisticated chef's workspace.

Regardless of their age, architecture or design, the common denominator of cabins is lifestyle. At the cabin, formality is out. We are free to do whatever we like in off-hours, and cabin design and décor reflect that spirit. Mostly, natural materials such as wood, stone, tile, natural cottons and other fibers are a preference in construction and décor.

In keeping with this relaxed and unstructured attitude, anything goes in decorating a cabin—imagination reigns. Do we really need to buy a new porcelain bathroom sink when we have a great old country bowl that could be used as a sink to fit into an antique country-style dresser that can easily be remade into a bathroom vanity? The ideas are endless.

In the earliest pioneer cabins, the entire structure was one room, including the kitchen, seating and dining area, and if there was no loft, the room was used for sleeping as well. In design holdover, today's cabin interiors continue to be open and only bedrooms and bathrooms are closed rooms.

Because the idea of the open living space is retained in today's cabins, cabin-specific kitchen design often means tying its design and décor to the rest of the house. Cabin-specific bathroom design might include keeping functional areas such as laundry and exercise nooks out of public sight in the great room layout. The following chapters investigate each component of a cabin kitchen and cabin bath and their role in the completed design process.

As photographers and writers, we have spent years shooting the work of architects, builders, decorators and homeowners, telling their stories in countless magazine articles. Much of our work is focused on log homes and cabins. This book offers you our perspective on cabin design and décor as well as expertise from manufacturing, design and building professionals. Homeowners we have come to know also weigh in, sharing their cumulative experiences, both good and bad. They offer what they learned early enough in the building process to produce great

results, as well as some tips they learned too late to make a difference.

This book offers suggestions on how you can reach the structural and design goals you set for your cabin kitchen and bathrooms. In the end, it is *your* cabin and should reflect your own unique style, your interests and the way you and your family live. There are no strict rules for your comfort; we offer you some ideas and tips—both practical and creative—on the best ways to get the optimum pleasure from your cabin kitchen and bathrooms. The rest is up to you.

Surprisingly, traditional décor works well in a log setting. Rich color and bold stripes enhance the beauty of the wood.

ARCHITECTURE
and
ARCHITECTURAL ELEMENTS

Architecture is as much a part of décor as furnishings.

Facing:
This soaring and dramatic window sets the design tone for the rest of this large-scale kitchen.

Choices of windows, doors, ceilings, flooring and fireplaces are as key to design as they are to structure. Nowhere in the cabin is that more applicable than in kitchens. This is because in the kitchen we have the added effects of environmental issues—heat, dampness, fluid spills, extreme light changes and heavy traffic—more than in any other part of the cabin.

The choice in architectural elements is usually between man-made and natural materials. A third possibility is factory-enhanced or engineered products that take natural materials and further fabricate them for more efficient use. One can consistently opt for one kind over the others, or mix and match.

Trade-offs abound, but generally, man-made materials are less expensive: aluminum window sashes are cheaper than wood; hickory floors are natural looking but more expensive than linoleum; bead board ceilings are more costly than drywall. That's just the beginning. Maintenance is also often higher with natural products that show the wear and tear of time and use.

THE CHARM FACTOR

For some, a cabin is a living organism that should reflect time passages. They love the patina that aging natural materials produce and aren't interested in collagen-like, man-made architectural elements. Others want a maintenance-free environment in which to live part- or full-time and will opt for whatever products will efficiently get and keep them there.

This is a personal and subjective call and there are aesthetically pleasing and sound structural methods either way. But know what you're getting into. If the salesman or builder says, "It really does look like the real thing," you should look with an objective eye—does it really?

Even if it doesn't look like the real thing and you'd rather have the practicality of lower up-front cost and less maintenance time and money, then there are dozens of manufacturers turning out thousands of great products for the choosing.

A polyester shirt can look good and feels almost like cotton—but not exactly. Some people, however, would just rather not iron, so they opt for the synthetic. It's the same in houses. What architectural elements one chooses often depend on the cabin. Vinyl-clad sashes can clash with the wood on a 200-year-old cabin, whereas on a contemporary milled log cabin, they can blend and offer practicality and a trim look. Sometimes the style of the structure itself suggests which choice to make.

In our travels across the U.S. photographing and writing about the nation's best and most interesting cabins, we learned that those people who invested the greatest effort in researching the products that work for them were the ones who, over the years, were the most pleased with their decisions.

Finally, while it's great to find the most knowledgeable and skilled building professionals, it is essential to be able to communicate with them intelligently about their suggested options for your cabin. You need to keep your own goals firmly in mind and learn about the materials and products that will get your cabin where you want it to be. The buck stops with you. In the end, it is you making decisions about what is best for your cabin, your budget and your lifestyle.

WINDOWS & SKYLIGHTS
LET THERE BE LIGHT—AND LOTS OF IT

Driving across the back roads of rural America, from where the idea of the American cabin springs, we have seen many early cabins and farmhouses both deserted and still inhabited. Some of these houses are more than 150 years old. These buildings have enormous charm but offered little more than basic shelter to those who lived in them. When those cabins were new, glass was rare and expensive and most of them originally had only one or two tiny windows. This was both good and bad news for residents of these usually dark and less-than-opulent homes; the small windows didn't let in much light, but they kept out winter winds, blustering snows and marauding bears.

Although today's cabins—antique and new, modest and grand—strive for the same rustic

HIRING PROFESSIONALS

BY GINA BATCHELOR ☞ PRESIDENT, LOGHOMESOLUTIONS.COM

Unless you're Davy Crockett living in the woods or one heck of a great builder/designer, you can't build or remodel and decorate your cabin kitchen and bath all by yourself. Sooner or later, even if you are doing the hands-on, down and dirty labor or the decorating totally on your own, you will need help. It is entirely possible (despite numerous nightmare tales from friends and relatives) to have a positive and fruitful working relationship with building and design professionals.

Hiring professionals can be overwhelming. After all, how can you be certain they will do a great job at a fair price and stand behind their work? There are never any guarantees, but if you do your homework and use the following steps, you will avoid many construction and design pitfalls.

Many of these suggestions deal with hiring contractors and subcontractors in the building trades. However, most of these same tips also apply to hiring interior designers and/or kitchen and bathroom planners.

HIRING CRITERIA

Some of the things that are most important when hiring a building or design professional are that he/she has the ability to listen and to partner with you in solving problems along the way, as well as to be honest and fair. Whether you are hiring a general contractor to oversee your entire cabin project or a job-specific subcontractor, there is little variation in the hiring process. Before you hire anyone, you will want to have at least three bid proposals in hand. The most efficient way to receive bid proposals from prospective contractors is to prepare a bid package. Your bid package should include the following:

- ☞ Invitation to bid: a letter that details the scope of your project and includes the project start date, the deadline for returning bids and the construction schedule or work schedule
- ☞ Architectural plans, pictures or patterns, where applicable
- ☞ A sample contract
- ☞ Deadline for returning bids
- ☞ Information sheet for bidders
- ☞ Contractor's license number, where applicable
- ☞ Bonding & insurance information, where applicable
- ☞ References

Each contractor you invite to bid should receive an identical package. That way you ensure that everyone is bidding exactly the same job. Make sure that you receive your bids by the deadline and that they include an itemized list of labor and material charges. Time and material bids have a tendency to escalate above and beyond what you may expect, so you will want to ask for fixed bids.

Be wary of very high bids and very low bids. These are usually red flags. A high bid can be the result of a contractor who may have a full workload and is willing to take the job only at a premium; however, do ask him or her why the bid is significantly higher, as the answer may be a valid one. A low bid is usually the result of someone who doesn't understand the scope of your project, which could cause problems once work begins. Once again, ask your questions and ensure that the reasons are valid.

(continued p. 9)

Three floor-to-ceiling windows installed in the dining room bump-out provide an abundance of light in the kitchen prep area.

appeal, most cabin dwellers are more than willing to sacrifice architectural accuracy for sunshine and a view. We have run across only a few die-hard purists who today install small windows in cabins, whether new or historic. Most of us prefer great swatches of light pouring in, especially into the kitchen. Given the vast number of companies manufacturing windows designed for optimizing the view as well as enhancing insulation, cabin owners can now have both style and energy efficiency.

With bids in hand, you are now ready to begin your selection process. For large and costly projects, thoroughly investigate at least three to four references for each contractor you consider. The references should consist of clients for whom the contractor has provided services in the past five years. Depending on the type of work you are hiring for, a simple phone call to the client may be enough to ask your questions. However, if you are able to arrange visits to the homes of the references, you'll be able to view the contractor's work. It is important to interview the contractor's references without him or her present so references can speak more candidly.

Important Questions to Ask
☛ Did the overall project run smoothly?
☛ If not, what went wrong?
☛ Did the project finish on schedule?
☛ If not, what held it up?
☛ Were the initial estimates accurate?
☛ If they went over budget, where and why?
☛ Was the contractor helpful in solving budget or layout problems?
☛ Was the contractor helpful in making suggestions or proposing ideas you had not thought of?
☛ If so, were his or her explanations clear and logical?
☛ Was he or she frequently present on the job?
☛ Have you had any major problems with the home during the time you've been occupying it?
☛ If there has been a problem, did the contractor follow up with you in a timely manner?

CHECK THE CONTRACTOR'S CREDENTIALS & AFFILIATIONS

Although there are many good contractors who do not affiliate themselves with industry organizations, it is a question you should ask. If they are affiliated, this affords you the ability to check with that organization and see if the contractor is in good standing. However, your decision on which contractor to select should not be based on this type of credential alone. You should also check with your state Attorney General's office about the prospective contractor or company.

SELECT A CONTRACTOR WITH EXPERIENCE

Without a good contractor, your major investment can quickly turn into a nightmare. Before hiring your contractor, make sure you verify all his or her work experience.

More Questions to Ask
☛ Whom did he or she apprentice with?
☛ How many homes has he or she been involved in?
☛ How many years has he or she been working on homes?

There's nothing wrong with using new contractors as long as they have verifiable credentials in their industry. Choose someone with proven experience.

THE CONTRACT

You selected the contractor with whom you are most comfortable. Now it's time to sign the contract. Most contractors have a standard contract that they use; however, you should be able to write in any changes that you feel necessary and that are agreeable to both you and your contractor. Below are some items that should be included in your contract:
☛ Start date
☛ Finish date
☛ Payment schedule

If there is anything in the contract that you don't understand, then don't sign it. You must understand every aspect of your contract to ensure that your project runs smoothly. ¤

The concept of cabin windows has changed dramatically over the last few years. There are myriad design possibilities in windows, given the huge variety of sizes, shapes and framing available. Windows are now as much a cabin design factor as any other architectural element in the house. Not only can we see the outdoors through windows, but we also make the view a part of our cabin by bringing the outside in.

The prevalent thinking is that today's cabin owners have sited their homes in places where there are special views they want to incorporate into their cabin design. They choose windows and placement as much, or more, for the views they frame of the outside as for their interior look. Window manufacturers are catering to that aesthetic.

Instead of one small sheet of glass stuck in a wood or log wall, there are now at least five basic kinds of windows available in almost any size required. Those are double-hung (can be raised and lowered from both the top and the bottom sill), casement, awning, slider and fixed (or picture) windows. Single-hung (those that only slide up from the bottom while having fixed tops) are still available for the vintage market but are no longer in great demand.

Casement and awning windows are hinged. They open with one side swinging out and operate by turning a handle; a casement is vertical and the awning is horizontal (where the glass swings up). State-of-the-art manufacturers have designed casement and awning windows with foldable handles

Both attractive and practical, small bay or "garden" windows are gaining popularity in kitchens.

THE KITCHEN FOOTPRINT

CUSTOMIZE YOUR CABIN KITCHEN TO FIT YOUR LIFESTYLE

BY HEATHER CHONG ☞ KITCHEN DESIGNER, McLEAN, VIRGINIA

When designing a cabin kitchen floor plan, the most important factor to consider is the way in which the kitchen will be used.

☞ Are there multiple cooks in the home, and do they tend to work together?

☞ Do they entertain?

☞ If so, do they hire help for larger gatherings?

☞ What types of foods do they prepare?

Cabin kitchens are much more than places to cook. They are where every good party begins and ends and where the family spends much of its quality time together.

Kitchen footprints have evolved to suit new uses. For years, the proverbial "triangle" stood its ground in kitchen design. This design pattern refers to a triangulated configuration of stove, refrigerator and sink all within steps of the cook. The basis for this approach to design is sound; however, it does not take into consideration the ever-changing role of the kitchen in a home, and especially the role the kitchen plays in a cabin.

In a small space, the triangle remains the best approach and is actually inevitable. However, in large kitchens with multiple cooks, well-meaning friends and helpers, and/or professional assistance for large gatherings, a single triangle alone does not seem to serve everyone's needs.

One approach that works well in cabins is to create multiple smaller, task-oriented workstations. This allows room for several people to work at once without getting in each other's way. One such useful station is a food prep area. Ideally, this is sited between the refrigerator or main storage area and the main cooking area. It should include a small sink, eliminating the need to use the main cleanup area for washing your vegetables and cleanup from preparing food. In some cases, there may be use for a secondary cleanup station with a sink and possibly a second dishwasher.

One size and shape doesn't fit all. Kitchens are all used differently, so why shouldn't they be individual in design? The term "custom kitchen" suggests that you should have the ability to make the space fit your family and individual cooking style. With all the advances made by appliance and cabinet manufacturers and builders, there is no reason not to customize. ¤

that do not interfere with blinds or other window treatments.

The kitchen presents a particular challenge in that the placement of windows can compete for space with appliances. We frequently see casement windows placed on the same walls as countertops, since they crank out easily when one needs to reach across twenty-five inches of counter space to open and close them. In this way, casement and awning windows are good options in kitchens where ease of ventilation is important. Double-hung windows are particularly difficult to access over counters and other kitchen work areas.

Awning windows, because of their horizontal

configuration, are most often used over glass doors, above fixed glass. They are sometimes the window of choice because they can be opened when it's raining without water pouring into the house. Window designers suggest that awnings and casements not be placed in a kitchen that faces a deck or patio if opening them can become a hazard to people outside.

The best look for a house, according to architects, is that windows of a similar style be used on the same side of a house. In other words, don't install double-hung windows with multiple panes on the same cabin face as single pane casements.

As a more inexpensive alternative to awning windows, where access to opening them is not an issue, most manufacturers produce sliders, which, as the name indicates, simply slide back and forth horizontally. They look the same as awnings but don't incorporate the expensive gear mechanisms.

There are many manufacturers of new windows, and most building contractors can steer you to the brand that will best suit your budget and design.

Facing:
Easy-open casement windows over the sink
bring in fresh air as well as sunlight.

Large windows, with the style repeated
on the same wall in the dining room,
add consistency to architectural design.

Unless you are a construction professional or have hands-on building experience, purchase windows, whether old or new, with the help of somebody who knows exactly what they are doing. However, as with all areas of investment, it pays for you—the consumer—to be as knowledgeable as possible.

An interior stained-glass window brings in light; it is cleverly installed in a space divider between rooms and is a strong design benefit.

Aside from window style, another decision is what materials should frame the glass: all wood, wood on the inside and vinyl or aluminum clad on the outside (eliminates the need to repaint the exterior every few years), or clad inside and outside (even lower maintenance, but not quite as natural looking). There will always be innovations in windows, as there are with other structural and architectural elements. Pella, one of the major window manufacturers, has recently begun offering a fiberglass product that they say is the best thing since sliced bread. They might be right about that, but since this product is only now becoming available nationally, the jury's still out.

There are a number of trade-offs involved in each window-frame style. According to Bernie Herron, an engineer with Cardinal Glass (a major producer of glass for many window manufacturers), "window framing is critical to insulation." While he emphasizes that "glass e-coating is invaluable for its insulation properties, the structure of the framing is just as important." Today, almost all state-of-the-art insulated windows are filled with argon gas instead of air between the panes. This gas gives just a little extra boost to the insulating properties of windows that are e-coated.

Herron feels that wood framing has the best insulation properties, with vinyl being comparable. Aluminum clad—whether extruded (which, when painted, gives a natural wood-like appearance) or rolled—is not quite as effective when it comes to creating a barrier against extreme climates.

Wood sashes are generally more expensive than aluminum. (Vinyl is the most economical.) However, many feel that wood provides the best look in a cabin, even though it requires a greater level of maintenance. Manufacturers that promote factory baked-on paints on wood sashes offer warranties for up to ten years. For unpainted sashes that the contractor or homeowner paints, maintenance is definitely higher. You could be looking at repainting these sashes every three years or so, depending on your climate.

In an ocean environment, the salty air does terrible damage to wood and aluminum, and experts agree that vinyl—which may not look as natural when juxtaposed with log and other wood materials—holds up better under seaside conditions. If you have the time and/or money for ongoing maintenance, then wood sashes at your seaside cabin could be your choice. But then again, if you like wood at the shore and choose to use it, but don't have the time and money to maintain it properly and often, you just might have to grow to love the "shabby chic" look on the outside of your cabin.

There are also a great number of architectural remnant windows available in salvage stores and antiques shops. They look great, especially in a cabin; but proceed with caution when considering whether or not to install them. If you don't know a great deal about construction, take a professional shopping with you. In addition to the often-important insulation properties (such as sealed panes, e-coating, argon gas and solid sealing between the glass and sash) you may be forgoing, be sure that the windows are plumb and square and not warped or liable to cause construction difficulties.

The best advice when building or refurbishing a cabin is to check in with local window distributors and ask which kind of framing holds up best in your particular climate.

After you've gone through the maze of technicalities in terms of materials, insulation and all the other bedeviling jargon, other decisions involve the aesthetics. Today's options for windows also include panes,

Facing:
A multipaned window, paired with similar cabinet doors, suggests antique architecture and provides that extra bit of detail that creates a design paradigm.

Multiple wood-framed windows can make today's cabins bright and airy.

known as grilles, that are solid to the sash or that snap in and out. The benefit of the solid grille is that it looks like an antique window, and those with snap-in grilles—no matter how much manufacturers deny it—don't have the same authentic look. However, windows with snap-out grilles are less expensive and, once the grilles are out, far easier to clean. There are myriad options for numbers of panes or just one solid piece of glass. It all depends on what style you prefer—single-pane contemporary or multiple-paned old-fashioned.

The possibilities offered by window manufacturers for configuring panes of glass within a window sash are seemingly endless. Taking time to make the

Don't forget skylights. They can provide additional ventilation as well as expand the feeling of bringing the outside in.

appropriate choice for your cabin is time well spent, as window style and design is major to the appearance of the entire home, inside and out.

THE SKY'S THE LIMIT

Skylights add to the window possibilities, providing a feeling of light and air in areas of the kitchen where placement of windows is not possible. They also add that extra burst of light; it's easier to cook when you can see what you're doing. Skylights can also bring a sense of spaciousness needed in smaller kitchens and, when properly installed, should not leak or affect the interior climate.

These skylights are either fixed glass or ventable; those that open can aid in air circulation, often needed in kitchen areas. Ventable skylights can be purchased either with a mechanical handle that one turns (there are specially made extension poles available for those set in extra-tall ceilings), or they can be hard-wired so they open and close electrically by using a wall dial. Manufacturers also sell roll shades that allow control over the amount of light entering from above.

THE DENOUEMENT

Windows, the hackneyed saying goes, are the eyes to your home; they present your "look" to the outside world—and frame that world from inside your cabin. Choosing appropriate windows for the kitchen and throughout the rest of the cabin is one of those decisions that—once you've spent the time researching the technicalities and the design styles—you'll find has been well worth the climb up that twisting, turning learning curve.

WINDOWS
KEY QUESTIONS TO ASK

BY ANN MAYER ☞ MARKETING COMMUNICATIONS COORDINATOR, KOLBE & KOLBE, WAUSAU, WISCONSIN

Ask your distributor where products are manufactured and what their track record is. Find out what type of product is suitable for your environment. Distributors sell these products every day and generally know if a clad product will hold up better than a fiberglass or wood. Find out about all the available options. Today there are more choices for consumers when considering products, from different designs and colors for hardware to different grille patterns and wood species.

If you do not ask these important questions, you are likely to get the standard and perhaps less-than-expected products; or, just as bad, you might pay for a lot more than you need or want.

I. *When shopping for windows, research warranties:*

  A. Ask your local window distributor for help. Usually distributors are familiar with different brands and can help you make an informed purchase.

  B. Find out what warranties are available on various products, and if they are prorated and cover parts and labor.

  C. Ask what the warranty is on the material that is used to construct the window. Most distributors should be able to provide you with written warranties for the products they sell.

  D. Read over warranties carefully so you know exactly what is covered and for how long. Many times different items on a window have different warranties.

II. *Checklist of environmental questions you should ask:*

  A. What type of glass is used in the window or door?

    a. Who manufactures the glass?

    b. What is the glass filled with—standard air or argon?

    c. Does the glass have a low e-coating on it?

    d. What is the U-value of the glass?

  B. What types of screens are available? (Some screen materials hold up better than others in particular environmental conditions.)

  C. Are storm windows needed in your locale?

  D. What hardware options are available?

    a. What colors and styles are available?

    b. What is the material from which the hardware is made?

    c. Will it deteriorate or discolor?

    d. What is the warranty on the hardware? Is it prorated? Is labor covered? ¤

DOORS AND ENTRANCEWAYS

YOU STEP ONE FOOT INTO MY KITCHEN AND . . .

Of all the cabin kitchens we have photographed, we have rarely seen one that is a closed-off room. Cabin kitchens—almost by definition—mean cooking areas that are open to the great room. Noah Bradley of Mountain Construction in Virginia has been rehabbing antique log and timber-frame cabins for more than twenty years and has had the same experience: "In all the years of cabin work, I don't think I have ever seen a walled-off kitchen." There is industry-wide concurrence with this perception. Floor plans of most of the new log home companies seem to take a cue from these old designs and maintain the kitchen as open to the rest of the cabin.

Early on, by necessity, when cabin square footage was at a premium and heat conservation was even more of an issue than now, cabin kitchens were an open-space extension of the living area. Now the inclusion of the kitchen into the overall great room is designed by choice; cabin floor plans still follow the ancient traditions.

Cooking at the cabin has become a social experience—the cook wants to be part of the fun that the rest of the group is enjoying. But there's still the need to separate the space and keep from displaying dirty dishes and smoking pans to the rest of the house.

Still, the space is defined by some kind of design element. We have seen any number of creative ways to achieve this. One method is to alter the kitchen ceiling and flooring materials from those used in the rest of the great room. For example, the kitchen could have a pressed-tin ceiling while the rest of the open-space ceiling is beaded board. Space-defining barriers such as open cabinets or screens are also effective in establishing room boundaries.

We've seen kitchen entranceways highlighted by dropped ceiling partitions between the cooking area

Facing:
An open floor plan keeps the kitchen a part of the rest of the great room.

Steps and railing provide kitchen boundaries, but the space is still open to the rest of the house. These are but a couple of the many ways you can open individual spaces to each other while still maintaining the integrity of each area.

Log posts and the arch provide delineation while maintaining an open kitchen.

Facing:
French doors to the deck add to an open feeling. They provide fresh air and easy access to serving outside, which is part of what cabin living is all about.

and the rest of the open cabin space. Beams or drywall can create this as long as the material used is consistent with the overall architecture of the rest of the cabin. If the ceiling is beamed, dropping the beams lower than the others in the house is one way to define the kitchen area. If walls are Sheetrocked, then a Sheetrock drop is appropriate.

These dropped-down areas can create open shelving for displaying collectibles and old cabin architectural artifacts that would fit well into the wooded charm of a cabin.

The sky (or the ceiling) is the limit when it comes to imagination and creativity in defining the kitchen space. One clever home designer placed antique corbels in each corner of the entrance to the kitchen, between the ceiling and the wall, in order to create a subtle but noticeable space definition.

IN THE MOOD

Solid partitions and doors are necessary to access and separate the kitchen area from utility rooms, closets, laundry rooms and pantries adjacent to the kitchen. It certainly kills country cabin mood to see dirty laundry on the washer or listen to sneakers bouncing around in the dryer. Here pocket, bi-fold and shutter doors are popular as space savers. Depending on placement, swinging doors are also useful to separate these spaces from the kitchen.

As for which door styles and construction to select from the thousands of designs offered in catalogs and at home centers, one can opt for hollow doors that cost less but lose something in the design translation. They lack that substantive feeling that many cabin owners prefer. Solid doors cost more, but most construction and design professionals recommend them not only for their aesthetics but also for their soundproofing qualities.

If they are within the kitchen area, try to use similar—or at least complementary—design patterns on the interior doors that are within view of nearby cabinetry.

IF IT'S TOO HOT IN THE KITCHEN . . .

Floor plans often lay out a kitchen that opens directly to the outdoors or with a dining area that accesses a deck, porch or patio. Here, too, door designs become a consideration in cabin kitchen planning.

Climate conditions of the locale permitting, we want to see as much of the outdoors as possible from the inside of the cabin, so it's no mystery why

all-glass doors have become somewhat of a standard. In terms of materials and technique of door construction, much of what applies to windows applies to doors as well. It is no accident that many window manufacturers also make doors.

Based on where doors to the outside are placed and how visible they are from the cabin exterior, window and door designers suggest using the same style of framing for the doors as for the windows that are nearby. If, for example, you choose grids on your windows, then it would be appropriate (but not necessary) to install glass doors that also have grids.

Additionally, because of the amount of space the glass doors occupy, insulation and solid construction are certainly critical elements. All the major window manufacturers produce glass doors that marry their window products in style and construction. Consistency in aesthetics and climate control should be a determining factor.

Traffic pattern and door placement go hand in hand. Too many homeowners have said, after the fact, "If I'd realized I wanted such a large table, I never would have put that door there," or "Putting that door on this end would have made it easier for me to get into the kitchen." In kitchen design there's no such thing as too much planning.

Facing:
An open arched wall separates the kitchen from the rest of the great room. The open door leads from the kitchen to the rear deck. Note the consistency between door and window styles.

Homeowners never complain about too many doors or windows.

GLASS DOOR CHECKLIST

**BY ANN MAYER ☞ MARKETING COMMUNICATIONS COORDINATOR,
KOLBE & KOLBE, WAUSAU, WISCONSIN**

Before buying a glass door, consider the following:

☞ What kind of view will it frame?

☞ A sliding door vs. a swing door: What will be in the room (or on the porch) that might interfere with a swing door?

☞ Which way should swing doors be hinged to open?

☞ What kind of warranty does it have? (Is the warranty prorated, does it cover parts and labor, and is the material that is used to construct the door also warrantied?)

☞ What types of screens are available?

☞ Is a storm window offered?

☞ Is the glass insulated? Does it have a low e-coating on it? What is the U-value of the glass?

☞ What are the hardware options (including warranties)?

Ask your distributor and/or contractor for help, keeping in mind the environment in which you live and how the framing will be affected by local weather conditions. Your exterior doors should be constructed as soundly as any structural part of your cabin. ¤

FLOORING

Nowhere in the design of a cabin is the tug between purism and practicality more dominant than in the area of flooring. And nowhere in the cabin is that decision more crucial than in the kitchen. Making decisions about flooring will depend as much on who is using the kitchen as anything else.

If it's just the two of you and you're both neat freaks who never spill anything and can attest to the fact that your refrigerator will never spring a leak during the time you're away from the cabin, then soft pine flooring might be the right choice for your cabin kitchen. If six kids, the whole gang from the neighborhood and two wet dogs are normal traffic in your cabin, and you're the kind of person who has nightmares about the first scratch on your new car, forget purism and head straight for vinyl floor coverings. Having said that, there are seemingly a million other flooring options in between. What is certain is that flooring is among the most important decisions to be made in the design of your cabin kitchen.

This flooring, albeit man-made, has a trim, clean look, and it is a snap to clean off muddy sneaker and paw marks.

Simple cabinets and equally
simple flooring make this
kitchen open and bright.

Facing:
This bold floor adds a huge textural
element to the log kitchen.

Practicality aside, flooring is also a major design decision. Do this little exercise: Look at a room with your hand over your eyes to block out the floor; you will see how much visual space the floor occupies in the room. The floor is far more visible and therefore more important to décor than one might initially think. Not only is flooring a decorative element, but it is also often used to divide spaces in an open-floor-plan cabin. While the rest of the open space might have wood flooring or wall-to-wall carpet, the kitchen may be set apart from the rest of the great room by use of a tile, vinyl or stone floor.

Cabin lovers are drawn to natural materials. In flooring, there are several options, all of which complement wood and log. In this department, popular choices include but are not limited to hardwood, stone, brick and tile. Each of these can again be subdivided into myriad types and styles; options are endless. In the hardwood category, industry sources, both manufacturers and distributors, all agree that oak is hands-down the most popular material for wood flooring in the U.S. It is a strong, highly grained material and is found in many cabins that have wood flooring. Maple, hickory, ash, pine and walnut are also woods usable for flooring.

A few checks and balances: dark stains show dust but look old-worldly. Maple (the stain or wood) glows if a light-colored floor is preferred and acts as a great visual counterbalance for darker log cabin walls. Pine, which can be stained any color, is a soft wood and scratches easily but can be found in widths up to twenty-plus inches. It is ideal for cabin dwellers who enjoy a textured antique look to their environment. Because pine lends itself to varied width options of

Facing:
Rugs add a practical element to flooring. They protect wood and other natural materials, make it easier on cooks
who are on their feet for long periods
and add pattern and color.

This bright, effective floor is actually bamboo, a grass product that
is growing in popularity.

Facing:
A throw rug on a wood floor, especially in potential
spill areas, protects the floor and makes it more com-
fortable for everyone.

the planks, it is reflective of early handmade floors. Dings and scratches are a wonderful part of the ambiance.

In the same general category, there is manufactured, prefinished flooring and unfinished flooring. Unfinished flooring means that you and your architect or builder decide on what natural wood is the preference and then those planks are purchased at a flooring store or a wood mill, planed and tongue-and-grooved for the best fit. The floor is finished or stained only after it has been laid. Prefinished material is factory sanded and stained and needs only installation.

Most flooring experts feel that wood flooring in kitchens is more difficult to maintain because wood and water are natural enemies. However, cabin owners who have insisted on wood kitchen floors feel that their careful care is worth every bit of time it takes. They love wood kitchen floors for their natural feel. Bamboo, which is actually a grass, is gaining popularity in the flooring market. There are also a wide variety of stains and finishes to consider.

In the category of stone and tile, choices are also extensive—some stone comes from quarries while other natural materials are manufactured into flooring products retaining their natural look.

FROM OUR FACTORY TO YOUR HOME

The good news about manufactured materials is that the production and design of man-made flooring has evolved and developed dramatically the last few years. Today, linoleum is not the cheesy material that covered Grandma's kitchen floor. The companies that produce linoleum are well aware of design-sensitive customers and have improved the look of their products.

Also not lost on flooring manufacturers is the fact that cabin owners crave natural materials. In response to this market demand, they offer engineered and laminated wood floors that combine

Traditionally patterned rugs suggest an antique look. Rugs soften lines, absorb noise and are increasingly being used in the kitchen.

The classic look of wood floors remains a popular choice for log homes.

"D" logs and wide plank wood floors match each other nicely and suggest a clean, uncluttered space.

THE BOTTOM LINE

BY CHRIS WOOD ☞ VICE PRESIDENT, SALES, HEARTHSTONE, INC., DANDRIDGE, TENNESSEE

As a designer and manufacturer of heavy timber homes, we find that wood floors complement the big beams in almost every home we build. However, keep in mind that although wood flooring can be effectively used in the cabin kitchen, slate, stone or tile might hold up better to traffic, moisture and dirt.

The width of the wood floor should be proportional to the size and scale of a room. Wide planks look great in large rooms. But wide planks (greater than 10 inches) want to shrink and cup, and availability is limited to softer materials like pine and fir. If the cabin will be used for entertaining in high heels, or if gaps in the planks are objectionable, I would not recommend wide, soft wood. Hardwood species in widths up to 5 inches are better suited for high-traffic, primary home uses.

The technology for drying large timber and wide wood planks is getting better and more economical every year. Most flooring should be kiln-dried in the 6 percent to 8 percent moisture content range before installation. Ideally the material should acclimate to the interior surroundings for one month before being installed during the winter months (when humidity is lowest).

Installation of wide planks should be done with screws, countersunk and plugged. Planks of less than 5-inch widths can often be toenailed with concealed fasteners. Glues and screws help keep it tight, but some purists will "float" the floor to manage the expansion.

Engineered (factory-enhanced natural) flooring products have also come a long way. Prefinished hand-scraped hickory with beveled edges in 5-inch widths is available and easy to install. This 1/2-inch-thick material is glued directly to the slab or plywood subfloor and is guaranteed not to shrink, cup or twist. I've been very happy with this rustic look in my own home, and the 2,300-psi compressive strength holds up quite well under traffic.

Sound transmission between wood floors can be controlled with acoustical membranes that are sandwiched between the subfloor and finished floor. Use glue or float the dimensionally stable floor and avoid nails, as they transmit noise below. Area rugs and upholstered interior furnishings help absorb the noise too.

Wood floors are a warm and comfortable way to finish any room. Materials with knots and defects add character and finish well.

Note: UV rays on southern and western exposures will fade everything—fabric, vinyl and even wood. Consider installing sun-tinted windows and patio doors on these walls to reduce the UV transmission. Use a quality sealer on wood floors to avoid "yellowing." Darker floors hide scuff marks and hold up better over time. Darker floors and lighter ceilings work well in cathedral spaces—most often found in heavy-timber cabins. ¤

and compress thin layers of wood to create a natural-looking flooring material that has become popular with cabin keepers who want the look of wood with the practicality of vinyl.

This and other man-made materials are readily available and cost-effective, and they credibly replicate natural materials while offering better and easier maintenance. Possibilities are limited only by our lifestyles and budgets. The ability of flooring manufacturers to improve the look and practicality of their products is a given in this industry, which consistently strives to offer new and dizzying variations and improvements.

In addition to the look of the flooring, consider wear and tear on the cook and helpers' feet. Plan to make the standing areas comfortable, and consider placing throw rugs in key areas where the house chef will be standing for long periods. If a kitchen is an extension of a great room or dining area, bear in mind how one type of flooring will marry with the other and consider the possibility of continuing the same flooring throughout two or more areas.

A log-beamed ceiling is consistent with the rest of the cabin and adds needed warmth and contrast to the drywall.

Facing:
Rustic beams, country-style furnishings and light fixture and the occasional decorative accessory make this kitchen look like an indoor extension of the outdoors.

CEILINGS: WHAT'S UP?

Ceilings contribute as much to the look of the cabin as any other architectural element. They can either unite the kitchen in design to the rest of the house or define the kitchen as a space unto itself. How much control one has of a cabin kitchen ceiling will depend on whether or not you are building a new cabin or rehabbing an older one. The choices in ceilings are relatively clear. Design options offer challenges and solve problems.

This wood-and-beamed ceiling offers an easy place to put a burgeoning basket collection and gives the room an intimate air.

LOWER THE BOOM

Low-slung kitchen ceilings, usually eight feet high, make the space feel intimate. These relatively standard ceilings make kitchens easier to heat and cool quickly. Choices of building materials include wood—either painted or stained—or painted drywall. Tile and pressed-tin ceilings are also available, and there is a great marketing push by manufacturers to consider these alternatives.

For the most light-reflective ceiling, the best choice is painted—the lighter the color, the more light is reflected into the room. This is a good thing in a kitchen where it becomes enormously helpful to see what you are doing. The relatively low ceiling does not afford the architectural drama of taller spaces, but it creates an enveloping ambiance.

For those who can't resist the warmth of wood as opposed to drywall, and who don't want wood strips, there are beaded board ceilings. This style is frequently found in old cabins from the mid- to late-nineteenth century, usually in rural parts of the country. This material consists of narrow boards onto which a rounded edge is applied or scrolled. It is then usually stained or painted. Beaded board is also often used as wainscoting or on cabinetry. If it's a look you are after and your cabin doesn't have it, it's an easy product to find at home centers or through contractors, who could apply it directly over an existing cabin kitchen ceiling.

A challenge in a relatively low-ceilinged room is that the kitchen area can feel squat and cramped.

This kitchen, with its cathedral wood ceiling, offers the best of both worlds: a sense of spaciousness and inviting comfort.

There are several solutions. The installation of skylights (see Windows) will bring in light and open the space. Also consider painting a lower ceiling white and matching the window and door trim to it. Paint can be applied to wood, beaded board and drywall. This will offer a crisp look and will be more light-reflective.

Vaulted or cathedral ceilings make room dimensions seem larger and airier. These two- (or more) story ceilings follow the exterior roofline and can be upwards of 16 feet high. They are often beamed as well. Most cabin builders who are designing structures of this style designate these ceilings as wood. We've also occasionally seen these vaulted ceilings in drywall, and they add a great surrounding sense of light, air and spaciousness.

However, the opposite of what applies to lower ceilings is true here. Depending on the source of heat and cooling in the house, it is likely to take longer to heat and cool vast overhead spaces. One solution is the installation of one or more ceiling fans that will push down warm air in the winter and circulate cool air in the summer. There are a number of fan companies whose products can easily be found in home centers or on the Internet.

On the other hand, if a vaulted or cathedral ceiling is what you want but you're concerned that it would make the kitchen feel too remote and cavernous, consider the use of window treatments to soften the space. Textiles in rich colors add warmth and can unify large spaces.

Considering that there is limited window space, this vaulted ceiling, with its height, skylights and white painted drywall, gives the airiest look possible.

A relatively modest-sized kitchen area is given that extra spatial "oomph" by a vaulted, steep-pitched ceiling. Note how the rustic warmth of the wood is highlighted by a floating, semiformal light fixture.

Rustic beams, whether or not they are structurally necessary, are hugely popular for their old-time look.

MIDDLE OF THE ROAD

A happy medium between the standard eight-foot-high ceiling and the expansive vaulted ceiling is to go somewhere in between. A wood-filled area with log walls and wooden cabinetry will feel more open if the ceilings are 9 or 10 feet tall instead of the standard 8-foot height.

CEILING ACCOUTREMENTS

Keeping in mind that most people who love cabins will cite their love of the warmth of wood as one of the reasons, it is certainly possible to build or apply wood beams to any height ceiling. However, in a cabin, especially a log cabin kitchen, one should consider the height of the kitchen when opting for beams.

Other ceiling choices include exposed beams that make the space appear rustic. They are enor-mously popular and some cabin keepers opt to cre-ate fake nonstructural beams that are set into the ceiling at specifically repeated intervals but are not needed to hold up the floor (or roof) above. Exposed beams offer a back-to-basics feeling, which is why so many cabin-minded people love them. In fact, nonstructural beams placed in ceilings need be nothing more than 4 x 4 pine lengths, textured, stained and then applied to the ceiling.

Styrofoam beams that can be stained or painted are also now being sold in local home centers. Most homeowners can manage the application of these. From a few feet away, these artificial beams can appear quite realistic.

Many people who have either cosmetically applied beamed ceilings or architecturally true beamed ceilings love them for more than the look. They are handy places to conceal track lighting, display collectibles, hang pot racks and discreetly tuck audio speakers.

Pot racks are almost a given in cabin kitchen décor. Not only do they spell out convenience but they can also add an old-fashioned, rustic accent that cabin owners find appealing. There are the standard pot racks that are available in most home-design and kitchen stores, but to add a dimension of creativity, many cabin keepers have cleverly used antique window grates and ladders to serve the same purpose.

Beams are also used to embellish kitchens with other design elements. Homeowners have hooked spice and dried fruit bundles from them, placed baskets and other collectibles on top of them and creatively engineered many other resourceful ideas for their use.

LIGHTING

BY CLAUDIA MITCHELL ☞ LIGHTING CONSULTANT, WASHINGTON, VIRGINIA

Proper lighting is among the most vital elements in your cabin; however, it is often treated as an afterthought in the material-selection stage as well as the budget phase. Lighting designers, architects and electrical engineers often use complex formulas to determine foot-candle (fc) distribution and fixture selection and placement. It can be daunting to the cabin owner, who often just leaves it to the professionals and then is unhappy with the outcome. This need not be.

In fact, we all have an innate knowledge of lighting. We have lived with it all our lives but probably not really noticed it. Now that you are planning your cabin, you might feel it is confusing and over-technical and decide to just put up some stuff that seems to blend well enough with wood. Don't do that. Spend a few hours in a lighting showroom that has a lighting lab and talk to experienced sales people, or at least go through a good selection of catalogs with the experts. This will be well worth your while. Ask for catalogs on recessed and track lighting and look in the back of each one. There you will find pages of simple drawings of cone-shaped diagrams that are used to show you how much light comes out of a fixture, how bright it is (measured in foot-candles), how many feet the light will go, and how big the spread of light will be at different feet.

Picture the tip of the cone being your fixture and the bottom of the cone being your floor or wall. If the tip is at your ceiling (or your beam), somewhere between the tip and the bottom will be your countertops, tabletops and desktops. You will also find guidelines for the optimum light levels for different areas or uses of space. These will help you decide, for example, how many fixtures it will take to light your kitchen. Carry a scaled drawing of your floor plan with you and refer to it as you shop for lighting. If this becomes confusing, ask a lighting expert in the store to help you shade in the size of the circle shown in the cone and coordinate it to your floor plan. (This can be fun!) You want to find a cone that has 10–20fc for general lighting, 20–100fc for task lighting and 20–50fc for accent lighting. Remember that your countertop will not be the bottom of the cone—that is your floor! These cones of light can be created by recessed or track fixtures. You won't find them for your chandelier unless it has a down light on it.

Overhead lights are not the only lighting your kitchen will need. This is especially true of cabin kitchens where the accent is often on wood, which is less light-reflective than other materials. You should also add under-cabinet lights for the best solution to lighting your countertops. As we get older, we need to

(continued p. 45)

Facing:
This pot rack, made from an old apple ladder and easily hung from the wood ceiling, is practical, imaginative and innovative and adds eye appeal.

Nothing suggests the appeal of hearth and home more than a fireplace, and no time is the wafting aroma of burning logs more seductive than when layered in with the perfumes of good home cooking.

FIREPLACES AND OTHER ELEMENTS

YOU CAN'T BEAT CHESTNUTS
ROASTING BY YOUR KITCHEN FIRE

An open kitchen hearth with a glowing fire is the essence of cabin lifestyle and provides that quintessential kitchen comfort zone. The appeal is huge, but the cost can also be vast. In fact, we have seen relatively few cabin kitchens—old or new—with any sort of fireplace or woodstove. They are so inviting that the only reason we can think of for seeing so few is that people feel intimidated by the cost

potential. Depending on choices for a kitchen fireplace or stove, money doesn't need to keep you from this great luxury.

On a scale of cost and ease of installation, fire-producing elements range from an old-fashioned wood-burning fireplace made of stone or brick to a cultured-stone fireplace, a gas or electric free-standing fireplace, a zero-clearance fireplace and a

look for a higher range of foot-candles to help our aging eyes work for us. Always use dimmers on your incandescent fixtures. The lamps will last longer, and you will be amazed at how wonderful the mood shifts in the warm glow of dimmed light, even in a kitchen.

Remember that you spent a lot of time creating open spaces, windows for views and exposed beams for structure and beauty; try to keep your lighting unobtrusive while painting your space with light. Beams are great locations for tracks to up-light the volume ceiling space as well as to down-light the room below. Try to side-mount track lighting to keep the track heads in the same plane as the beam and not hanging down below it. Even in a kitchen, utilitarian track lighting need not be obtrusive.

Track manufacturers make tracks in several finishes and track heads in very small scale. Linear lighting as well as rope lighting might also be used on top of the beams. If you use recessed lights, be sure to invest in sloped ceiling cans and trims. Get out the recessed catalog and look for the cones that have the measure-

ments for the height of your vaulted ceiling.

Extra note beyond lighting: A vaulted ceiling usually lends itself to having a ceiling fan installed. This is not the time to save money. Regardless of the style or finish of the fan, it should always have a powerful motor that will quietly run blades that have a steep pitch of at least 14 degrees; 16 degrees is even better. The fan catalogs you use for your research will give the motor capacity and blade pitch for each fan. Also, be sure to buy a fan that has a wall control that will reverse the blades. This is very important because it will allow you to take advantage of your fan in winter as well as summer. While it saves on energy costs, which some fan manufacturers report are reduced as much as 40 percent in the summer, it also increases your comfort. Out of the box, your fan is set for summer to create a wind-chill effect to cool you. When fall comes, reverse the blades and your fan will move all of that heated air out of the volume ceiling down to your living space. Because you invested in the wall control to do this for you, your 14-foot ladder stays in the storeroom. ¤

glass-fronted woodstove. Costs are not cut and dried in any of these categories, and prices vary extensively given the brand of stove or fireplace and prices of local raw materials and artisans' labor costs.

One thing is certain: if you decide to build a stone or brick fireplace in your kitchen, prepare to spend many thousands of dollars for an experienced stonemason or bricklayer. However, relatively new to the market is "cultured stone," a man-made concrete product that is impressive in its real rock look-alike texture and that stands at about half the cost of natural rock, both in the purchase of the material and in its installation.

Less costly is a cinderblock flue through which piping for a wood-burning stove is run. Some of these stoves actually have glass fronts from which the fire is visible. There are also gas fireplaces that produce real flames from manufactured logs and electric fireplaces that produce a wired—and somewhat artificial-looking—glow instead of real fire. These alternatives provide varying degrees of ambiance at a fraction of the cost.

Industry experts offer some advice about choosing which, if any, of these elements for your home. They strongly suggest that you determine just what function you want your fireplace or stove to perform. Is it for heat, romantic ambiance or both? A relatively new item on the market is the zero-clearance fireplace, which vents horizontally to the outside, eliminating the need for costly flues and chimneys. They don't look quite as authentic because their fireboxes are metal as opposed to masonry, but they offer a

This old hearth provided all the cook space the family needed when it was first built in the nineteenth century. Hearth cooking is increasing in popularity.

Facing:
The ultimate in cabin comfort is a fireplace with hearth.

A woodstove provides a huge comfort zone in a kitchen. Many are made today with doors that open so homeowners can enjoy burning logs as well.

Facing:
The gas fireplace, on the left side of the door, provides the warmth of a wood-burning fireplace without the logs. The old cook stove on the right is an irreplaceable heirloom in this early log cabin. There was a time in which the stove was the entire kitchen.

great trade-off in financial savings. These might be easier to install, as allowances for venting are a standard concern in building or renovating kitchens.

It is essential to check with a reputable contractor or stove dealer when contemplating any fire-producing element. The learning curve on the technicalities of types of fireplaces, stoves, stovepipes and chimneys is steep. Like so many other products now available in the home-building industry, there seems to be something new on the market every day.

Learning about the possibilities of having this element in a cabin kitchen is well worth the research. We have never met a cabin owner with a kitchen fireplace or stove who doesn't feel that it's the highlight of the room or regrets having installed it. The allure of a kitchen fire is so basic to our love of home and hearth that one should at least consider the possibilities that exist for installing one in your cabin kitchen.

THE LILYCROFT

LORD MASHAM
SAMUEL CUNLIFFE LISTER

TETLEY

FURNISHINGS

Y our cabin is an empty canvas. Because the kitchen is more than likely to be visible from the great room and vice versa, ideally the design and décor of those spaces should be planned at the same time. This is a challenge. The style of kitchen furniture—including both built-in and freestanding—as well as textiles, colors and design "theme" should, to some degree, coordinate with the look of the rest of the space that is visible from that area.

The choices for kitchen design are endless. We have seen constantly recurring themes, such as cowboy, southwestern and English cottage, in the hundreds of cabins we have photographed over the years. However, don't feel that you have to be pigeonholed into a category; cabins need not have a décor theme at all.

Color, with one main tone or shade and one or two accent colors, can be the entire theme of a room's design. Sometimes, as when decorating any room, the designer or homeowner chooses colors from a patterned rug, a bold painting or other strong element in the great room and carries them throughout.

Antiques add a warm dimension to cabin furnishings. Vintage country pieces are durable and often found at a greater financial savings than new pieces.

Facing:
Stone, log, pine beams and painted cabinets provide a variety of textures, tones and colors.

Most people who put effort into cabin décor recognize the very masculine feeling that wood brings to the look of the rooms. They can either choose to accentuate that masculinity by using earth tones, plaids and leather, or seek to deflect it by using softer colors and patterns. Many cabin owners ignore the visual cues given by wood or log walls and beams and install wood furniture of the same color and tone. They then add upholstered pieces of the same shade to create a singular monochromatic and potentially boring blend. We see this look often. Fear of color and contrast scares people into blandness.

The idea of coordinating the look of the entire open space of a cabin might seem overwhelming. However, once you have decided to theme or not to theme, or to coordinate by color, your decorating life will become easier. This actually narrows the endless kitchen décor possibilities that exist. You'll be grateful for these reduced and limited options and feel quite liberated.

CABINETRY

For pioneers and settlers living in early cabins, the term "kitchen cabinetry" was oxymoronic. This was because these folks had almost nothing to store. It didn't take more than one or two open shelves to hold a pot, a pan, a few dishes and a can of baking powder. The term *décor* applied only if the lady of the house curtained off these shelves with checked gingham fabric that matched the single window curtain.

Today, cabinets define the look of the entire kitchen because of the sheer amount of square footage, from ceiling to floor, that they occupy. Therefore, high-quality, well-constructed and finely designed cabinets are a good place to spend a major portion of your kitchen budget. Cabin dwellers need more storage, especially if they are in rural settings, miles from a quick trip to the market. Face it: we're a society of consumers and like lots of stuff.

WHAT A DIFFERENCE A CENTURY MAKES

These days, cabin kitchens are efficient working and cooking areas where we want and need maximum upper and lower cabinets with highly evolved and well-designed ways to easily reach and utilize every inch of space. At almost every level of the cost spectrum, today's kitchen cabinets offer many amenities, such as pullout drawers behind cabinet fronts, lazy-Susan configurations inside cabinets with easy-access storage in the back and think-of-everything compartments that include flip-out drawers for damp sponges and special nooks for cookie pans and trays.

Great cabin kitchens sport cabinet systems with rustic and antique styling and having the same efficiency as other contemporary kitchens. As for materials from which cabin cabinets are made, much of what is true for windows and flooring is true for cabinets. Most are made of wood and engineered wood products; pine, maple and oak are among the most popular. These can be custom-made to your specifications by local craftsmen. Depending on your locale and budget, this might be a good way to go. Employing a skilled carpenter usually brings top-level craftsmanship and generally insures that you get exactly what you want.

However, most contractors and cabin keepers buy their cabinetry at major home centers. Anyone who has ever been lost in the endless aisles of a home-center chain store knows that their inventories are vast. There are myriad producers of kitchen cabinets that offer a selection of cabinet designs, in a variety of woods and finishes, at a wide price range. Some brands are so well crafted they appear custom made. Unless you are

These cabinets are both contemporary and traditional. The contemporary feeling comes from clean lines; the design emulates antique styles. Note the glass-doored units above the microwave that are specifically designed and lit for displaying collectibles.

100 percent certain of what you want, you should send for catalogs and visit home department stores and kitchen stores. Invest the time to look over the huge selection of cabinet face designs, configurations and finishes. Some are solid natural wood and others have wood fronts with plywood sides. Almost all of them are coated for easy cleaning. Once you are familiar with the options, you will be able to make choices that will still satisfy you later.

Kitchen planning is tricky and errors can be expensive. Consider consulting a kitchen designer. Some home centers provide this service free of charge, but independent, Certified Kitchen Designers (CKD) offer more expertise and creativity and are an extremely worthwhile investment. They can breach the mazes of choices and help you arrive at a cabinetry plan that works for your cabin. They can assist you in choosing cabinets that will fit the dimensions of your kitchen floor plan and lifestyle.

Plate racks are old-fashioned in style while also being enormously practical.

New, built-in cabinetry set well below a soaring ceiling gives an airy atmosphere to this contemporary cabin kitchen.

Facing:
Open cabinets are as popular today as they were 200 years ago. As long as you are tidy, it's a great look.

PEEK-A-BOO

Certain cabinet designs convey particularly rustic or antique looks. Crown molding, glass fronts, plate racks and shelves for cookbooks and collectibles are all reminiscent of early cabin kitchen life. They are also elements that are visually effective in today's cabins.

If you just can't find what you like, you can install a very simple cabinet face and doctor it, making it your own unique design. Some ideas we have seen completed by the most clever and creative cabin keepers include glass-fronted cabinets that offer a wonderful rustic look. Some people, however, find they don't want the interior of these spaces open for inspection by the neatness police. One solution is to install small curtain rods on the insides, across the top and bottom of the glass cabinet fronts, and curtain them with fabric that matches either the kitchen window treatments or the primary colors of the rest of the kitchen and great room.

Open shelves full of dishes and pottery are practical and make a strong design statement.

Facing:
These homeowners wanted windows all around, so virtually all of their cabinets are "bottoms" to free up the space above to let in bursts of sunshine and the views.

We have also seen white cabinet interiors "wall-papered" on the tops, bottoms and sides with fabric or paper. When the dishes are set in the cabinets and the glass front doors are hung, the fabric or paper makes a great but subtle design statement. You can glue fabric or paper, or when the surface is totally without lamination, apply starch to the fabric and the fabric will adhere perfectly to the cabinet surface. When you're ready for a different look, you can just peel off the fabric and starch up another batch.

COLOR ME IMPRESSIVE

New kitchen design theory suggests that using more than one color cabinet makes an effective design statement. Upper cabinets painted hunter green look great when the lower cabinets and island are finished pine. You can also use more than two colors. Bold primary colors contrast happily with log and painted-Sheetrock cabin walls. Stark white cabinetry looks fresh and country bright. However, if you opt for these, think about what fingerprints will look like around cabinet handles and drawer pulls, because you'll be cleaning a lot of them.

White cabinets and a soft-toned rug give this room a coat of fresh and bright ambiance.

Facing:
These green cabinets add
drama to and highlight
wood surroundings.

Textures of log, stone and
smooth wood communicate
their own design language.

A great example of how
black cabinets can look
bold, not dark.

When you've made your basic decisions about cabinets and colors (paint or stain), you can pay some attention to luxurious accent points that, in fact, can make all the difference in the world: hinges and pulls.

Although hinges that are interior to the cabinet doors are mainly chosen for their strength and durability, you can also consider outies—hinges that rest on the doors' exteriors. They can be quite effective. With hand-wrought metal designs by craftspeople and manufactured ones in multiple varieties, the choices are limitless. The size of exterior hinges, of course, should be proportional to the cabinet door. When you see beautifully designed

Minimally visible hinges and pulls translate into clean, contemporary lines.

Small, Shaker-style knobs blend well and are a traditional classic.

hinges placed on richly colored or naturally toned cabinet doors, the effect is quite dramatic. However, drama may not be your raison d'être, and you may prefer to have the woodwork or colors on the cabinets speak for you.

Thought should also be given to the drawer and cabinet door pulls. You can choose to have these objects blend in and not be a focal point, or you can make them a consistent design statement about how you like accents in your environment. Like earrings, they can complement, dangle, surprise and add one more pretty feature, or they can take most of the attention. It depends on the face you wish to present.

These pulls emulate a late-nineteenth-century style.

Antique-style "H" hinges on cabinets help give a historic appearance to the kitchen.

FIRST THINGS FIRST

BY DON O'CONNOR ☞ DIRECTOR OF SALES & DESIGN TRAINING

WOOD-MODE CABINETRY, KREAMER, PENNSYLVANIA

Regarding cabinetry, among the major categories are ready-to-assemble (RTA), stock, semi-custom and custom. The purchasers assemble RTA units themselves; the cabinets tend to be stock—what you see is what you get. Successful use of RTA units calls for a bit of self-analysis: When you start jobs, do you finish them quickly? Are you prone to reading directions *before* you begin to assemble anything? If the answer is no, then six months later you'll have a stack of cabinet parts all over your floor accompanied by a highly annoyed family. Marriages have been threatened by less.

Semi-custom cabinetry tends to have higher-quality construction and a limited—but still highly adaptable—choice of customization. For instance, dimensional changes and modifications will be available, meaning the homeowners can get more flexibility with cabinetry specifically adapted to their needs and floor plans. Compared with stock or RTA units, they'll probably work better with specialized appliances such as commercial-quality ranges and fridges, which are more popular nowadays.

Custom cabinets may require a higher investment from the client, but they will have superior construction and a greater choice of door styles and finishes, as well as special finishes and colors. Furthermore, your designer can plan units to integrate specialized or imported appliances and even one-of-a-kind furniture units to coordinate with your kitchen and the great room.

Before making any decisions, I recommend you and your family do two things: First, think and discuss long and hard about what you expect from the project. What functional aspects are most important? What look or theme would you like the room to have? It's like Abraham Lincoln's remark, "If I had four hours to cut down a tree, I'd spend three of them sharpening my saw."

At the same time, think about the budget. Building and remodeling magazines constantly feature articles on this area. One issue had the same room with three different kitchen plans proposed—a good-better-best approach. The budget ran from $20,000 to $60,000 in the same room.

A designer colleague of mine always tells people, "Whatever budget you have in mind, double it." In fact, a good designer is likely to work out your budget up front, to avoid wasting everyone's time with a design that's either beyond your means or one that's within your budget but doesn't meet your needs.

Place yourself in the hands of a competent Certified Kitchen Designer (CKD). If you've just moved into your locale, ask them for references from previous clients. A good designer will bring a wealth of experience to the table and be able to make recommendations in your best interest to fit your budget and needs. ¤

COUNTERTOPS

Like all materials available in a cabin kitchen, countertop choices are vast, with trade-offs in cost, looks and maintenance. There are as many countertop "stories" as there are kitchens. Some swear by one material and others swear at it. How one material works in a specific kitchen varies according to usage, maintenance and how much upkeep people are willing to endure to enjoy the specific look of one material over another. We will try to sort out some of this.

Still, some people will feel that a particular material, regardless of what we say about it, presented problems for them. On the other hand, the very material that experts say is the least popular is the element some love best about their kitchen. Given that, we will do our best to examine a few of the most popular kitchen countertop materials. We are not attempting to cover every countertop available, just offering an overview and a place to begin.

These marble-style countertops are seamless, high style and enormously popular.

Harriet Finder, CKD, of Stuart Kitchens, a forty-plus-year-old kitchen-design firm serving Baltimore, Washington, D.C. and northern Virginia, offers suggestions on the good, bad and ugly of cabin kitchen countertops. "There are lots of great countertops from which to choose. It's a matter of finding the best product for your cabin kitchen use," Finder states. While some products are almost impervious to heat, water and scratching, they may be difficult to clean and look totally out of place in a cabin kitchen. Or they may also cost more than you want to spend.

As for cost, Finder learned that over the years, some less-expensive countertop materials such as Formica sell for so little that they're really out of the pricing equation but still available if budget is a major issue. Most of the materials that are now popular are fairly close to each other in price. This, of course, still depends on grade of material, color and edge detail. It can also vary a little according to geographical region.

Harriet Finder discusses some of the largest-selling countertops:

☞ **GRANITE:** The stuff is hard as a rock (the only harder material is a diamond) and cleans up beautifully. Once sealed on installation, granite needs only occasional resealing over the years. Darker colors have greater resistance to stains such as red wine. Finder suggests when used in a rustic setting, granite can be honed to achieve a matte finish. However, that process makes the material more porous and therefore a little less resistant to stain.

☞ **QUARTZ:** A crushed stone product, quartz is non-porous and therefore stain resistant. However, some people feel that this material in a cabin setting looks better honed for a matte finish, but then, as with granite, it will be slightly more likely to stain. It has all the benefits of granite. Silestone is a popular and well-known brand.

☞ **TILE (CERAMIC):** This versatile material is available in a huge variety of colors and textures and looks great in a rustic setting. It is absolutely heat resistant. It does have an uneven surface, which can make glasses and other small objects tip. Also, grout, the material between the tiles, is still not as stain resistant as the tile itself.

☞ **CORIAN:** This material is not as wildly popular as it was several years ago, but I still recommend it for its durability. One drawback is that it does scratch, but scratches are fairly easily removed, as are stains. Corian can also handle considerable heat.

☞ **STAINLESS STEEL:** This industrial-looking material is as close to perfect as possible for keeping clean and free from stains. It is literally maintenance free. You can even set hot pots on it. The negative here is that it does scratch and dent. In a cabin, this material can be a great visual counterpoint to wood walls and cabinets.

Wood is a classic and traditional material for counters. For those who love it, maintenance is well worth the effort.

☞ **CONCRETE:** These countertops are custom-made to fit your kitchen. The material is poured to fit a template made from your kitchen's counter configuration and then sealed after fabrication. It is extremely durable and heat resistant and doesn't scratch easily. However, concrete can stain from citric acid-based food materials. It has a great textured look reminiscent of a Tuscan-style kitchen; this can be effective in a cabin setting.

☞ **LIMESTONE AND SOAPSTONE:** People love these two natural products. Softer and more porous than granite, they offer an earthy, muted look but can scratch and require a little more maintenance than harder materials.

☞ **PAPER:** This is the hottest new kid on the countertop block. Long used in restaurants, these paper-based, fiber-composite surfaces are considered safe to use in food-preparation areas and come in a wide variety of muted, nontextured tones.

Other kitchen industry sources are enthusiastic about butcher block. Usually made from hardwoods such as maple, the jury is hung on this material that is the epitome of a great country look. Some feel that it is a high-maintenance product. It cannot take standing water or burns under hot pots and needs to be coated with mineral oil several times a year. It has a clean, rustic appearance and can be used to cut on, which is not recommended for other harder surfaces.

Facing and above:
In today's cabin kitchens, there's lots of countertop
space; it often wraps around and seems to go on for-
ever. Since you and your family will be working on it,
putting things on it and looking at it for a long time,
choose countertop materials with thoughtful care.

WRAPPING IT UP

No matter which of these one chooses for a cabin
setting, countertop material should be selected at
the same time cabinet style and finish selection is
made, so that the materials coordinate with each
other visually.

Harriet Finder suggests when selecting countertops or any other kitchen material, be aware of your
own preferences, tolerances and family's lifestyle
and needs. Try to realize what you want your home
to be. Do you find some scratching on countertops

In a galley-shaped kitchen,
this island adds extra space
for breakfast while creating
a little divider that separates
the work space.

Facing:
This kitchen has an eat-in
area as well as an island/bar.

Here the material on a modest-
sized island blends with flooring
and cabinetry for a trim look.

charmingly rustic, or does it drive you nuts? Do you mind wiping down fingerprints? Consider whether or not your home needs to look perfect, or if the natural wear and tear of living adds to the satisfaction of cabin keeping. Once you know what you like and need, you can make choices that best suit your way of life and create a cabin kitchen to match.

ISLANDS

Cabin ambiance is really about getting back to basics; the essence of hearth and home—what Bob Dylan called "shelter from the storm." Early cabins were often just one room, with a woodstove or fireplace, a couple of rocking chairs, one or two beds and the good old farm table on which food was prepared and eaten. The farm table was also the place of family activity: children's studies, card games and reading.

Today's lifestyle has upped the ante on "basics." We're used to more, so what seems minimal to us now would have astounded early cabin dwellers. Our cabins expand on their simple theme. Today's cabin kitchens have adapted from their ancestors and have added comfort and twenty-first-century style.

For example, kitchen islands now take the place of the farm table. They also act as room dividers, storage centers, cooking stations, dining tables and general hangout locations. The island has become such a staple of kitchens, especially in cabins, that some families have two. However, an island is still, in fact, a table—one that may be attached to the floor, one that may be on wheels and may or may not incorporate a sink, stove and/or dishwasher. No man is an island—but any table could be.

In the vast kitchen market, there are so many designs, styles and functions of kitchen islands that the choices are staggering. Generally, the island design is somewhat related to the style of cabinets, but it doesn't have to be. We have seen designers and cabin keepers effectively use the island or islands as a design counterpoint to other woodwork in the kitchen. If the cabinetry is wood tone, then the island will often be painted or stone-sided, becoming a design focal point for the room and also functioning as an architectural point of departure from the kitchen to the rest of the great room.

Vince Achey, vice president of sales and marketing for Plain & Fancy Custom Cabinetry notes the following trends:

☛ **SMALLER ISLANDS (NARROWER AND LONGER):** In the past, islands had that bulky "aircraft carrier plunked in the middle of a kitchen" look. They were so wide you couldn't reach anything in the middle. Today, they're smaller.

☛ **COMPACT ISLANDS:** Some homeowners opt for two compact islands that are highly functional and more agile. For example, one island may house a combination of appliances: dishwasher,

New island, old concept.
This island is a new take on
traditional and historic use.
With its antique legs and
grain bin and veggie storage,
this piece is reminiscent of
Granny's kitchen or an old-
time country store.

This simple island affords a
wine rack, an element that is
growing in popularity.

Facing:
This island does it all. It sup-
ports the cooktop and provides prep area and storage
space.

 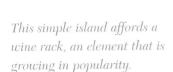

Above, below and facing: Three entirely different cabin kitchens with islands that fulfill similar needs. They all have shelves for cookbooks and other niches that provide multiuse storage in these all-purpose centers.

sink, range or refrigerator drawers. The other may be mobile, on rollers, with a work surface on top and open storage below. This second island can also work as a prep or service area for hors d'oeuvres and drinks.

☞ **FURNITURE-LIKE ISLANDS:** No matter the size or shape, islands often take on furniture-like traits with feet, turned legs and bead board sides.

☞ **MORE COLOR:** This is a good place to add a splash of color, adding life to a space with a minimum of design risk. For those on a budget, custom color on an island is a great option.

☞ **VARYING SURFACES:** There is high interest in granite, limestone, concrete and wood surfaces that include butcher block, cherry, teak and maple.

Harriet Finder also offers the following thoughts about island planning.

If you opt to plan your own kitchen without consulting a kitchen designer, keep in mind that while there are no hard-and-fast rules about the ratio of island size to room dimension, there are some good rules of thumb to consider.

☞ Plan the size of your island around the kitchen space you have, after you account for cabinets.

☞ Make sure you allow plenty of negative space in which to navigate around the kitchen.

☞ Leave at least 42 inches of space between work areas. If your kitchen is huge, you should leave more than that amount so that the island doesn't become enormous. However, if you have a tiny kitchen, you can diminish those 42 inches a little to make sure the negative space is ample for movement and to accommodate the aesthetics of the room.

The island has often taken the place of the farm table, as have creative pieces of newly designed furniture.

Facing:
A do-it-all island provides storage, a food prep area and surround for a second sink.

FREESTANDING FURNITURE

In cabin decorating, it's like the restaurant slogan that says, "No rules, just right." However, after photographing hundreds of cabins, we found some basic ideas that worked for cabin keepers who created visually effective and unique cabin kitchens.

It's not the money—it's knowing where to spend it. One of the best and most effective ways we have seen dollars provide the biggest bang is in the area of freestanding kitchen furniture. In most cabin kitchens, cabinetry and the center island or islands usually take up most of the floor space. Freestanding individual pieces of furniture also have a place in this area. Furniture gives the room individuality and offers the homeowner the chance to create a unique kitchen.

Individual, well-made cupboards that are not built-ins, but that contrast with the cabinets and island, create a timeless, original look. This is even more effective if the piece is antique. While antiques shopping for the uninitiated might seem

Facing:
An old-style farm table that can be both a work and eating surface adds creative possibilities for the cabin keeper.

This antique Hoosier cabinet is a decorative catchall for a variety of collectibles. It also offers great storage space.

An antique chest of drawers works well as a freestanding piece at the entrance to the kitchen. Juxtaposed to an island/counter, it helps divide the kitchen from great room areas while adding storage space.

A whimsical stool/table configuration provides a shot of individuality in this log kitchen.

like a better way to burn bread than using a faulty toaster, it need not be the case. Often, size for size, a good antique piece, found for a reasonable price, will be financially comparable to, or better than, new high-end manufactured cabinetry.

Also, consider the island stools: If you have wood or log walls and wood cabinets, especially if they are not stained or painted to contrast with their background, consider using stools of an entirely different material. Think wrought iron, leather, wicker or even stainless steel. There is drama in contrast.

We repeat the mantra: There are no decorating

Simplicity works by pairing clean lines in both cabinetry and an equally plain but contrasting table.

These homeowners painted an antique bookshelf filled with their lovely transfer ware to match their kitchen cabinets.

This is a wonderful combination of contemporary chairs with a classic farm table. Whimsy and good design distinguish this kitchen.

shalts and shalt nots. However, because design and décor can be expensive and are an expression of one's own personal, albeit perhaps quirky, taste, one might be afraid to go out on a design limb. Don't be. The cabin is the place for it. If you always wanted a hanging swing in your kitchen, try it in the cabin—even if it is your full-time home. Cabins welcome the individuality of their owners. Families who have put their individual and creative stamp on their cabins seem happier when they're in them.

UPHOLSTERED FURNITURE & TEXTILES

Cabin words: *comfort, rustic, historic.* These are some images to live by when designing and decorating a cabin kitchen and extended great room. Of course, there are no set rules when it comes to furnishing a cabin, but few people would want them if relaxation and comfort were not the end goals in owning them.

Cabin comfort conjures up images of overstuffed, down-filled chairs; sofas and love seats; low tables; soft lighting and sunshine streaming from windows and washing over woody walls and floors. Furniture in much of the cabin is part of the open kitchen and looks best when coordinated. Design coordination is a desirable goal and reaching it isn't easy.

We have found that people are often so over-whelmed by the endless possibilities of cabin décor that they choose monochromatic color schemes in their furnishings that are almost identical to their wood or log walls. They do this believing that by using browns and beiges, they will bring out and enhance the color of the surrounding wood. In fact, those colors do the exact opposite. Using textiles and furnishings that match log and wood walls tends to make the furnishings disappear because there is no contrast in tone and color, and all of it tends to become one visual mass.

There are at least two ways to go in selecting fabrics in a cabin setting. One way that can be extremely economical is to haunt flea markets and auctions for vintage fabrics. Over the past few years, wonderful old textiles have caught on with

Facing:
Recipe for comfort: a down-cushioned wicker chair in a cabin kitchen.

This is a groom's apartment in a log barn and, as such, is the epitome of multitasking under one roof.

ROMANCING YOUR CABIN WITH FABRIC

BY PAMELA MAFFEI-TOOLAN ☞ VICE PRESIDENT OF DESIGN, WAVERLY LIFESTYLE GROUP

Owners of cabins are in love with the look, feel and romance of wood. The textiles they select for their homes should elicit the same reaction. The way a fabric feels is as important as how it looks and lasts. Waverly, one of the largest American manufacturers of textiles for home décor, recommends the look of natural fiber for use in decorating cabins. Their base textiles run from the simplicity of cotton duck to special ornamented jacquards that offer patterns with depth and a sense of richness.

In cabin great rooms, chairs and sofas in stunning statement prints serve to underscore the richness of wood walls and beams. Deep, gathered skirts on slipcovers add softness—a romantic balance to the intensely masculine ambience of log and wood spaces. In most cabins, Roman shades, pulled up during the day, or valances in a charming fabric will complete a room, yet leave windows open to nature and sun.

Connect rooms by color, especially in homes with great rooms and open plans. With navy and jewel tones in the living room, the kitchen might pick up either or all of the colors—or various shades. Fabric collections make textile coordination easy, both within one room and throughout the house.

COLOR AND PATTERN

There is a tendency for cabin dwellers to dress rooms in brown, beige and other neutral shades, but the monochromatic effect can lull the eye away from the beauty of the wood rather than enhance it. In fact, the right contrast between decorative elements in the room and the walls helps accentuate the wood. Instead, for upholstery, on kitchen chairs and for window treatments, for example, choose colors that have an earthy base, in combination with a classic print. Look for fabrics that are printed on neutral grounds and consider some of the wonderful reds as well as the desert-jewel colors prominent in many of today's fabrics.

As for patterns, fresh ticking stripes and ginghams are perfect for rustic settings, as well as florals and charming vintage motifs. Paisley is another pattern at home in a cabin. Bold but still tailored, classic paisleys come in a wide variety of patterns and colors and add traditional elegance to a cabin setting. Tailored menswear motifs, such as plaid and foulard, also look handsome in cabin surroundings, as do textural metalassé and woven cotton textiles reminiscent of knitted woolen blankets.

Bold country-striped slip-covers accessorized by vintage fabric-covered pillows on this loveseat create a comfortable country look in an otherwise simple and contemporary kitchen.

cabin keepers and decorators and can't necessarily be snatched up at the low prices of a few years ago. However, these drapes, originally created for the large windows of Victorian and other early homes, were made of the finest cottons and silks and can often still be found far beneath the cost of new fabrics. Remade into window treatments and throw pillows, these early textiles blend perfectly with the spirit of log and wood walls. If you prefer newly made textiles, fabric stores are full of material created by manufacturers sensitive to the demand for textiles with old sensibilities.

However you go with textiles, new or old, paisley, checkered or toile, the fabric in your cabin kitchen is as much a design statement as anything you put in that room. Textiles have the considerable benefit—in time, energy and money—of flexibility and changeability not offered by cabinets, windows and other major investments. So, in a couple of years, if you're bored or just want something fresh and new to brighten up your cabin kitchen, it's a lot easier and cheaper to change the upholstery on a chair than to junk all your almost-new cabinets and appliances. Not only are curtains easier to take to the dump than a refrigerator, but new ones provide the most change for the least money.

APPLIANCES

I t doesn't take a degree in design to know that every working kitchen needs a sink, stove and refrigerator. Today's kitchen offers so much more. This chapter discusses which appliances will work and look best in your cabin. There are, of course, many more appliances that you may want or need in your cabin if it is a full-time home rather than the occasional weekend getaway. However, even in the most basic kitchens, most people opt for a dishwasher. Then, contingent on the size of the kitchen, the very latest among the top-ten wish list of appliances are refrigerated drawers to be located at strategic points in food prep areas and workstations. The wine refrigerator/cooler is another gourmet appliance that is growing in popularity. Automatic mixers, food processors and cappuccino, espresso and pasta machines are growing in popularity as kitchen must-haves. Considerations such as lifestyle, number of people in the cabin, how much company visits and how serious a foodie one is determine which appliances are essential to create three square meals a day. In this chapter, we will stick to basics.

These standard black appliances fit in well with the kitchen's design.

Facing:
This major stove is for serious food preparation—perhaps even for the local army; but it might be overkill if it's just for one or two on the occasional weekend.

Which appliances you choose depends largely on the footprint (see chapter 1) design of the kitchen you made when you designed the entire cabin. In this chapter, we will focus on design and décor elements of appliances rather than the technical virtues of which individual brands to include in planning your kitchen.

We offer the following criteria on which to base the types and styles of appliances that work best in a cabin with an open kitchen floor plan.

IT IS WHAT IT IS

It is possible and totally acceptable to purchase basic large appliances and install them with only minimal design planning or financial investment. You can buy a refrigerator from $400 up and a stove for about the same. Of course, these appliances can also cost thousands of dollars each, but if you just need to keep food cold and then cook it, you can do that without stretching your budget. Most appliances come in a small variety of colors: black, white, off-white and stainless steel. One exception to this is sinks, which many manufacturers offer in a variety of colors, including red, blue, green and even patterned designs. It's fun to choose a sink that will pick up and highlight colors you may have chosen for accent walls and window treatments.

If your taste identifies with the parents of baby boomers, you might still be able to find avocado, canary gold, and that all-time favorite of the fifties, pink. But don't say the suggestion came from us.

There is nothing wrong with furnishing your kitchen with the basics. Surrounded by an attractive arrangement of cabinets, even visible from the rest of the great room, visitors aren't going to be shocked because your cabin kitchen contains appliances.

Kitchen design experts suggest that selecting all your appliances from one manufacturer is easiest, but that may not solve all your needs. It is fairly simple to coordinate designs from different makers. (We said "simple," not "quick and easy.")

IT IS WHAT IT USED TO BE

If you are history or antique motivated and decide to focus considerable money on appliances, look into vintage pieces—old appliances reconfigured and brought up to date. Kitchen designers say that this is a growing portion of the appliance industry. John Jowers, president of Antique Appliances, a preeminent restoration company of vintage appliances in Clayton, Georgia, agrees. He finds that cabin owners are particularly drawn to an earlier era of focus on home and hearth and long for visible reminders of the "good old days" in their kitchens.

These early stoves and refrigerators were made at a time prior to endless rows of cabinetry and kitchen islands. They were designed and manufactured as stand-alone pieces of furniture, not to be part of a decorating ensemble.

Appliances from the 1910s to the 1960s can be refurbished to be fully functional and have become good investments. Like restored early automobiles that are not modernized to have all the bells and whistles of computerized vehicles, these period refrigerators and stoves are refurbished to their original working condition. Because they were built when the mind-set of consumerism emphasized durability and artfulness, even in the kitchen, it's no wonder that people—especially those who love their cabins—opt to install them. Cost, as with any well-functioning mechanical antique, is high—but then so is the appeal.

An old-fashioned stove set against a stone wall adds an historic look.

If you want late-nineteenth- and early-twentieth-century style that functions at a twenty-first-century level, consider reproduction vintage appliances. They might not be the real thing, but many people want the look without an expensive price tag. There's also a time consideration. Obtaining a refurbished vintage major appliance isn't only expensive, but having Granny's honeymoon refrigerator or stove (or the one you find for a "steal" at the local thrift shop) put in working order through Antique Appliances or another reputable firm can take a year or more. Even cabin

The clean lines of an old-styled stove complement the stream-lined cabinetry.

Facing:
An antique stove in the great room gives a historic and rustic feeling to the entire area.

owners who revel in the slow-down lifestyle of an antique kitchen will lose enthusiasm and patience searching out and then waiting for that perfect vintage appliance.

Many reputable firms manufacture reproduction—look-alike appliances with all the extras expected in a modern refrigerator, stove or toaster. They are more costly than the traditional appliances, but they do add that one-of-a-kind stand-alone look.

There are numerous options available in the design features of these retro-style appliances (brass

This stove looks like Grandma's but cooks like today's.

Facing:
An industrial-style stainless-steel stove and hood (which matches the light fixtures) play well against wood cabinets.

trim versus chrome, etc.) and they are ready to go. However, they are generally more costly than contemporary appliances and they don't have the authentic antique quality, either in looks or value appreciation, as the real vintage items refurbished for daily use.

Other trade-offs: Reproductions of vintage appliances tend to offer the same state-of-the-art efficiency as new models sold at large home stores, (e.g. automatic timers, self-cleaning options). Although cleanability wasn't necessarily stressed, authentic vintage items offered a variety of cooking features rare in today's models, such as two ovens for simultaneous baking and broiling.

Nowhere, it seems, is there more potential for trade-offs than in the kitchen.

At the risk of overstating our case, we maintain that it is easy to fall into woodsy or old-timey overkill when designing a cabin kitchen. One of the best ways to underscore the warmth of wood is by using contrasting materials against it. This holds true in appliances as well as in color coordination. Stainless steel stoves, sinks and refrigerators, as well as small appliances such as mixers, toasters and coffeemakers, enhance rustic-looking log walls.

We've seen many log and timber-frame kitchens with a genuine country look dramatized by stainless steel appliances in the cooking area. It works.

Stainless steel, however, requires higher maintenance than other surfaces. Being shiny and reflective, it tends to show every scuff and smudge. However, it

is cleaned easily with special products and, when in tip-top condition, you can see in the reflection how beautiful you and your kitchen really are.

GOING UNDERCOVER

Although freestanding appliances and built-ins have their appeal, cabin owners don't always want massive refrigerators announcing their presence, nor are dishwashers and trash compactors the most attractive items in any décor.

If you prefer to hide appliances so that you and only you know which door hides the refrigerator and which drawer holds the dirty dishes, most major cabinet manufacturers, as well as smaller custom shops, offer panels that match the rest of kitchen cabinets in style and finish to fit over the fronts

and/or sides of these appliances. New state-of-the-art configurations are dramatically accelerating. Today, one can bury dishwashers and compactors in islands as drawers, or in almost any shape and place imaginable.

Wood-Mode, a high-end firm based in Kreamer, Pennsylvania, not only offers a comprehensive line of standardized panels for appliances that match the rest of the kitchen's cabinetry but will also do custom work to fit preexisting cabinet surfaces.

Don O'Connor, one of Wood-Mode's lead designers, says that most appliance manufacturers offer trim kits for adhering front and side cabinet panels. "It's a matter of discussion," he explains, "between the consumer and the cabinetmaker to decide which brand of appliance is most appropriate for the choice of panel that blends in well with the kitchen design." O'Connor warns that many appliances won't accept panels that cover things like handles and dials, and advises that there are only a couple of manufacturers that make the kind of products that work well as built-ins without having the ostentatious chrome-heavy handle jutting out. The cost of appliance panels equates to just about the same per square foot as the rest of the cabinet surface in the area.

DESIGN
and
DÉCOR

The fun begins when the unfurnished interior of the cabin is ready for your personal decorating touch. The time you invest in this effort represents the culmination of years of planning and saving hard-earned dollars. Giving it the look that you always envisioned is a challenge. In fact, the nitty gritty of putting it all together may not be as easy as when you made sketches on the backs of napkins, on yellow pads or in your daydreams.

Cabins, like all other houses, are essentially organic; the best of them grow and evolve. While it's possible to have the place fully decorated in just a few weeks, the best advice of countless cabin keepers and design professionals is to take it slow.

See the large picture first. Instead of trying to decide which piece of furniture goes where, or even what style of furniture "fits" in a cabin, think about what makes you and your family comfortable—the most comfortable you and they have ever been. This is probably the feeling you want for the cabin. As experts have said, the kitchen is likely to be the heart of your cabin, and it needs at least as much design and style consideration as the rest of the house.

Ladder-back chairs add charm to this log kitchen area.

Facing:
Simplicity rules this well-designed kitchen. Simple pine cabinets are seamless adjacent to log walls and ceiling. Note the use of alternative material in the tall chair at the island.

COLOR

ZOOMING IN

When you're defining your special "look," color is as good a place to begin as any. Once again, taking the counsel of design professionals and the owners of the best-looking cabins, when it comes to color, take clues from your own choices. Look at the tones you choose for your clothing, those you prefer your spouse to wear and what you select for your children. If you find that your wardrobe tends toward bold colors and patterns, it is likely that these shades make you feel good; if you find neutral shades in your closets and drawers, you have already chosen what feels best for you. Of course, you are not preordained or sentenced to this color standard, but if you haven't a clue where to begin looking for ideas, this is a place to start.

You probably made some color-oriented decisions when you chose kitchen cabinetry. If your choices veered toward blending similar shades of wood for cabinets and flooring with the logs or wood of the walls, you can still opt for brighter or bolder accents. These can be picked up in window treatments that will match or blend with treatments in the rest of the great room. Another good source for a shot of color or pattern is in the cushions for the tall chairs at the kitchen island.

Texture is another design element not to be overlooked. If you have chosen a lot of wood in the kitchen for what kitchen planners call the *hardscape*, such as counters and cabinets, try varying it with painted stools or stainless steel or even copper

Facing:
Adirondack-style chairs maintain the texture of this cabin kitchen.

Color is the name of the game here. Lush red cabinets and warm pine floors covered in creative country hooked rugs are simple design elements that equate to high style.

cookware, pot racks and other ancillary food-prep paraphernalia. Stone, tile and glass elements also work well with wood.

ZOOMING BACK OUT

There are also the design themes discussed earlier: Old West, with cowboy collectibles; English cottage, with floral patterns and painted furniture; Adirondack, with twig furniture and plaid upholstery; Country Americana, with cotton and home-spun checks and plaids; and Arts & Crafts, with linear furniture and earth tone–shaded upholstery, to name a few. If any of these is your style in the great room, the look can be carried through in the kitchen with choice of color, pattern and texture in window treatments, rugs, pillows and upholstered furniture.

We have seen many cabin kitchens with down-stuffed easy chairs, love seats and porch swings. It certainly adds to the feeling of the kitchen being the heart of a cabin.

This space is nothing more than simple and inviting— and that's plenty.

For some, designing a cabin kitchen may feel overwhelming. There are countless kitchen planners who can either offer a perfect turnkey room or simply be available for suggestions and guidance. If you decide to go with some help, check with friends whose houses you admire. Interview the prospective design professional to make sure that both their taste and personal style fit your aesthetic and personality. Some people want to be told exactly what to do and how to do it. This kind of approach might feel overbearing to others. Kitchen design professionals can help you wade through the morass of possibilities, both technical and creative, and help solve problems with an experienced set of eyes. Remember who works for whom, whose cabin it is and who will be signing the checks. You will be living in that space. Make sure, even if the professionals like or dislike something that appeals to you, to buy and install only what you like. Most professionals are client-sensitive and respect the relationship between designer and cabin keeper. However, some can be quite authoritative—don't be intimidated.

⊲⊳

THE DOWNSIDE OF A WONDERFUL KITCHEN—FAMILY AND FRIENDS MAY FEEL SO MUCH AT HOME IN YOUR KITCHEN THAT THEY MAY OPT NOT TO VISIT ANY OTHER PART OF THE CABIN. THIS BAGGAGE COMES WITH THE TERRITORY; BE PREPARED.

⊲⊳

WINDOW AND WALL COVERINGS

Although most cabins have wooden walls, some cabin keepers feel that wood everywhere is too much of a good thing. To combat the brown blues, they have come up with inventive ways to introduce other colors, patterns and textures. This is especially

IT'S ALL IN THE DETAILS

BY MICHAEL BUCHANAN ☞ INTERIOR DESIGNER, NEW YORK, NEW YORK

Good design principles apply to all rooms regardless of the architecture or design style. From my perspective, the most successful rooms, from cabin to high Victorian are spaces that are not "matchy matchy," or areas that do not stick to one particular style. It may not be true for everyone, but for me, balance is everything—elegant formality next to primitive creates the most personalized spaces. The concept of mixing and matching periods, finishes and city versus country pieces has been mastered by Europeans but is only now becoming recognized as an effective interior design method in the States.

If great design doesn't come naturally to American families trying to put rooms together, it seems to run in our national culture. In the late nineteenth to twentieth centuries, America's wealthy relied on European culture and decorative arts and furnishings to create instant ancestral heritage. Unfortunately, they often missed the subtlety of the Europeans and overly exaggerated elegant European design and style. Hence, we see a lot of overblown robber baron museum houses—the homes of our wealthy ancestors, who often missed the decorating boat altogether.

The best twenty-first-century American design incorporates a variety of styles. The most creative American designers know how to balance styles using baroque and primitive furnishings in the least likely settings. An eighteenth-century, elaborately carved, gilded chandelier obviously belongs in an historic eighteenth-century high formal interior; but a great designer could effectively place that same chandelier in a post-and-beam, primitive barn or American log cabin. By using a keen eye in scaling proportions and by having sensitivity to texture and tone, a contradiction or contrast in styles can be used effectively.

To understand this concept better, let's relate this to a successfully dressed person. Simple attire, such as a simple black linen dress for a woman, is plain, but add a one-of-a-kind silk scarf and a unique piece of jewelry and the whole outfit makes a tremendous statement. For a man, a crisp white shirt, classic blue blazer and fabulous formal silk tie worn with blue jeans also makes a visual statement. These presentations immediately send the message that even though the person is dressed down, they have a flair for elegance and sophistication. The same concept holds true for cabin interiors.

A cabin kitchen need not be designed in one flavor. Adding one or two splendid accent pieces—formal, historic, high camp or contemporary—can dramatically change the entire effect of the space. The idea of dressing something up or down is a trend that has been used in design for decades. Why not have luxuries like down-filled cushions and pillows in your weekend cabin, reflecting the style you may have in your urban dwelling? No one needs to know if your sofa was a yard sale find for $75 or designer-made for $7,500. Polished cotton or crisp white duck slipcovers create instant high style.

Just because our interiors appear to be understated doesn't mean they have to appear cheap. Understated elegance is the most sophisticated of all design concepts; the success is all in the details. ¤

important in kitchen design so the kitchen space can tie in to the décor in the rest of the great room.

Patterns, textures and colors on some walls are also effective because, by contrast, they emphasize the wood quality of the adjacent walls and the ambiance of a rustic interior. Wall color and wallpaper can define room spaces in an open cabin plan. Painted walls or wallpaper that extend beyond the immediate work area of the kitchen into the breakfast nook or dining area not only coordinate the architectural continuity of the open-space design but also serve to blend that section with the rest of the great room. Conversely, by papering or painting only the business end of the kitchen, one can create a space that clearly defines and separates the kitchen from the rest of the room.

Additionally, wall and window treatments can play a role in making the kitchen area either more sophisticated or more informal. They can also be a supportive backdrop for collectibles or artwork you might want to put in your kitchen area.

Classic stripes make an elegant design statement in small kitchens.

This bold wallpaper is a strong contrast to log walls in an extension of the kitchen area pictured below.

This inviting kitchen, extending into a breakfast nook, is a comfortable hangout.

Tile adds a bold and unique style to this timber-frame galley kitchen. Sometimes you can do more with a smaller space than a larger one.

Bricks, baskets and a butcher-block island bring a special designer look to this kitchen.

APPROACHES

One couple compromised on the idea of a log cabin: he wanted it; she didn't. Their solution was to build with "D" logs (flat on the inside), and then pickle them, giving them a white-wood look with wood texture showing through. This became the ideal surface on which to hang their art collection.

We have also seen interior drywall walls that have been painted, wallpapered, tiled, or covered in cultured stone. Tiling or brick-facing one section of wall, perhaps behind the stovetop or ovens, can add a visual and textural dimension that would give the entire surrounding area a focus.

For less-permanent results, rotate a collection of

large quilts to hang on kitchen walls. This will provide color and texture. When you want something different, switch quilts or remove them altogether.

As for window treatments, there are two schools of thought here. In a cabin, the installation of curtains and drapery are certainly as possible as in any other house. But for the sake of informality, just a swag of fabric that coordinates with other colors or patterns in the great room (helping to make that architectural and spatial connection) is enough to soften a window and relieve the all-wood look of the space.

Some cabin owners who have wonderful views and plenty of privacy wouldn't dream of hanging anything at all over their windows. Their décor choice: nothing but nature.

In a small space, consider a simple color scheme; it makes for bold design and a larger-feeling room.

DISPLAYING ART & COLLECTIBLES

Almost everyone collects something, from fishing lures to lunch boxes, ceramic cats to old cookbooks. Surround yourself with the things you love; the cabin is the place to let it all hang out and hang up. The kitchen is the one task-oriented room in the cabin and is therefore filled with appliances. It is also a living space and a room for gathering friends and family. Adding collections of some of your favorite things gives the kitchen a sense that it is also a social center.

If you opt to maintain wood walls in your kitchen, you have created a collection-friendly medium. One of the best things about wood walls is that it's easy to put nails in them. If you decide you don't like your arrangement or wish to add or subtract, wood walls are very forgiving. Hanging shelves—as well as collectibles and artwork—is easy on wood. You don't need to worry about bruising your knuckles looking for those elusive studs behind drywall or covering up your mistakes if you miss them. You can create the arrangements for wall hangings by first laying objects in a pattern on the floor to see the effect and then tacking them to the walls. This is particularly effective in the kitchen where so many of the objects are utilitarian.

A collection of American folk art adds personality to this bright, open kitchen.

WHAT TO HANG OR SHELVE

There are myriad collections that you may already have started or those that would be appealing that fit the realm of kitchen-related items. These would include antique and vintage cooking implements such as red- or green-handled spoons, graniteware, spatulas and chopping implements, yellow-ware bowls and white ironstone pitchers. Almost any object with some graphic value hung or displayed in multiples can be effective wall or shelf art.

One certainly need not feel consigned to

Why not consider the kitchen a living area and another place to enjoy your collections?

Facing:
A collection of antique spoons, forks and spatulas
adds to the historic feeling of this cabin. Be sure
they're hung securely before you sit in that chair!

The cabinetry is brand-new, but a mélange of collec-
tions, placed with studied casualness, gives this
kitchen a relaxed, rustic and historic ambiance.

kitchen-related items. Non-kitchen objects graphically arranged on a kitchen wall can provide a whimsical visual break. Another avenue of collecting to consider is objects that tie directly to the cabin's locale. For example, if your cabin is in lake or river country, having a collection of water-related objects—e.g., fishing nets hung on walls and baskets on beams—brings a provincial dimension. We're not suggesting you need reminders of where you are; it's just that this collecting and display approach emphasizes to you and your guests that your cabin is at home where it's sited and you love your environment.

We've seen everything imaginable on shelves and walls and even placed on beams: pond boats, decoys, baskets and bottles; there are no rules or limits. Also, in the two-dimensional realm, nothing could be more perfect than an oil painting, poster or advertising sign on a log wall. Remember, it's your cabin—fill it with the things you love and you'll never go wrong.

The homeowners' collection of antique arrowheads is now the highlight of their custom island.

The cabinetry, designed for displaying collections, keeps the space uncluttered while giving it personality.

Facing:
A homeowner's basket collection and farm-style furniture add texture and personality to this newly built cabin kitchen.

This Maine cabin kitchen is the perfect spot for a pond boat with masts that don't quit.

The china displayed on top of the cabinet was actually a soap-box premium collected by the homeowner's grandmother.

These vintage utensils are arranged in a clever kitchen corner display. (Vintage is a polite word for things that aren't yet antique and are still affordably found at yard sales and flea markets.)

A collection of vintage items massed in a small space makes a large statement.

COLLECTIBLES AS DESIGN

BY AVRAM FINKELSTEIN & PHIL MONTANA ☞ GOLD GOAT ANTIQUES, RHINEBECK, NEW YORK

The kitchen isn't just a room; it's the soul of a cabin. That's why it's the perfect place for a personal design statement and to share your sense of play. Regardless of its size, everyone likes to congregate in the kitchen. Following are some design ideas for kitchens of any size:

☞ If your kitchen is large, consider decorating with trade signs; they're bold, they're graphic and they add color. Oversized shop signs—like a bottle, scissors or a mortar and pestle—add dimension to a room and look great hanging from a beamed ceiling. We once found an oversized store-display potato peeler to hang above a client's sink and a 24-inch fork and spoon that looked great over a range. Trade signs range in price from $20 to $50 for small wood or metal farm-stand signs, to several thousand dollars for nineteenth-century gilded asphalt signs or hanging trade signs.

☞ Long grocery store signs are ideal for filling the dead horizontal spaces above kitchen cabinets, over doorways or in arched areas tying into the great room. Smaller painted signs can be grouped in small clusters to unify spread-out patches of wall.

☞ If your kitchen is smaller, grouping your collections will help reduce clutter. You might also consider using wall pieces to preserve needed counter space.

☞ Fishing or twig baskets are compatible with an Adirondack-style cabin, and they can serve double duty in a kitchen when they're wall-mounted as utensil bins or used as tabletop cutlery or napkin holders.

☞ Camp canoe oars are colorful fillers for slivers of horizontal or vertical wall. They're easier to find than Native American canoe paddles, and much less costly.

☞ Hen-shaped wire egg baskets are an inexpensive way to add sculptural detail to a country kitchen counter. Expect to pay $20 to $40 for one. If your sensibilities are more modernist, try hanging a group of round egg baskets with their bases against the wall, like an abstract sculpture.

☞ Another great accent grouping is a cluster of wall-mounted iron trivets. They're reasonably priced, easy to find, and they have an architectural quality that's compatible with either contemporary or traditional environments.

☞ Mounted antique cookie cutters can also add architectural interest. They're great clustered on a wall in large or small groupings, or museum-mounted as small sculptures to place on a window ledge, lined up across cabinet tops or over a doorjamb. ¤

Corner display shelves look trim and make good use of space. The wicker rocker fits well with the old-fashioned country feeling of this kitchen.

KITCHEN JOURNALS

Each cabin keeper has his or her set of challenges in designing an ideal kitchen, and the finished space reflects the time, money and creativity invested in meeting those challenges. The most unique kitchens we have seen have been decorating visions of people who used their own skill, time, energy and stamina to do some of the work themselves or at least were on hand to make sure their ideas reached solid fruition.

Following are the journals of two cabin keepers who each had a vision for their kitchens. They share how they achieved their goals. Each design meets their highly individual standards; each epitomizes the look they wanted. Both cabins are one-of-a-kind spaces bearing the stamp of their talented owners and each is an example of opposite ends of the décor spectrum: one an innovative take on country Americana and the other cutting-edge high style. Each of these rooms was designed with passion and is as different from the other as a kitchen can possibly be.

Don and Janice Mahaffey's creative personal touches make their kitchen unique.

KITCHEN JOURNAL

OPEN KITCHEN, OPEN HEART

BY JANICE MAHAFFEY ☞ DESIGN CONSULTANT, FIRESIDE LOG HOMES, ELLIJAY, GEORGIA

Our log home, nestled in the mountains of Ellijay, Georgia, is filled with natural materials direct from our own backyard. The first floor and loft total 1,380 square feet and are designed with forest accents surrounded by white pine logs.

During the planning process for building our cabin, we decided to incorporate an open kitchen rather than one that would be closed off from the family living area. Throughout the years, having both open and closed kitchen floor plans, we decided that cooking alone is no fun and being able to entertain family and friends from the kitchen would be an essential part of the aura of the home.

When you walk through the front door, the kitchen is straight ahead; therefore, we knew it needed to be not only attractive but well planned and workable. We designed the kitchen with a work triangle where the stove, refrigerator and sink are all within reaching distance.

During the building process, Don and I decided to install the tile on the floors, backsplashes and countertops ourselves. We were looking for a unique and warm look, so we used 18-inch-square tavertine tile with smooth edges. After sawing each tile in half, we then chipped off the edges of the tile with a hammer to give it a more rustic look. The tile was carefully set in place with a stained grout to match the tile floors and then sealed with Teflon filler. We used a coordinating tumble marble on both the backsplashes and countertops. The tile is easy to keep clean and looks presentable at all times.

Accent lighting was one of the most important features, not just in the kitchen but throughout the entire cabin. The lighting adds warmth and provides a room with personality; it creates a welcoming effect. It was very important to preplan for the electrical needs of accent lighting to avoid visible wires.

We installed rope lighting in the kitchen, near the floor under the base of the cabinets, to accent the tile floor. We used Puck lighting inside the antique glass cabinets where the log-cabin decorated dishes are displayed and underneath and above the upper cabinets to continue to accent lighting design and brighten the countertop and ceiling area.

All of the cabinets are made from white pine, just like the logs used to build the cabin. The kitchen countertops are trimmed in walnut. Since the kitchen is sited opposite the front door as you enter the house, we raised the counter to obstruct any undesirable kitchen views. We set the countertops 38 to 41 inches from the floor, not for any decorative purpose, but to accommodate Don's 6-foot 8-inch height. This makes cooking more comfortable for him.

To continue the forest theme, the cabinets are trimmed with twigs from the yard. All of the cabinet

(continued p. 118)

knobs are made from the same material. I sketched trees out of white pine and then cut out and mounted them on each cabinet door and on the front of the counter. This helped to bring the kitchen and living area together and create an attractive view when entering the cabin.

To add more rustic flavor to the kitchen area, we placed two sliding baskets in the pass-through space that connects the rest of the great room to the kitchen, in the lower cabinet area. Also visible when entering the house, the natural rustic baskets display vegetables and fruits that are accessible from either side of the counter. The fresh produce on display adds to the natural look of the room and, as Don makes fresh fruit juice, it was important to him that these items be easily accessible. Keeping this small space uncluttered was a challenge, so one solution was to install an appliance garage that keeps utilitarian electrical appliances accessible but out of sight.

Since our kitchen consists mainly of white pine with evergreen pine tree accents, we chose to highlight with splashes of red. We feel that the décor has a crisp and inviting country look.

With the combination of accent lighting, glass and tile cabinetry and bringing nature indoors, our tiny open cabin kitchen has become a favorite spot in our home. Whether cooking for ourselves or family and friends, we don't miss a moment together. ¤

Michael Warner and John Mastriani's high-style country kitchen involved a risky leap into imaginative design.

KITCHEN JOURNAL

OUR COUNTRY CABIN KITCHEN

BY MICHAEL WARNER AND JOHN MASTRIANI ☞ **FREDERICKSBURG, VIRGINIA**

When we first built the cabin, it was a weekend getaway; a place where we could hide out, sink into big chairs, read and relax as far away from everything as we could get. We wanted each room to be a warm space that described our collections and lifestyle. We followed no set pattern of décor. If anything, we wanted the interior to have a European flavor. The kitchen design evolved, as did the rest of the cabin.

Then, when this became our full-time home, we wanted it to retain the same ambiance and appeal as when it was just a weekend getaway. While we loved the idea of our rural, rustic setting on six acres of woods, we couldn't deny ourselves the kind of urbane design elements to which we were accustomed in our full-time city home. For us, then, it was a matter of combining both.

Our palette was the woods that surrounded our cabin and the wood of so many of the interior walls. We wanted a small exterior entrance to appear as part of the environment, and then when the front door opened, there would be this big expanse of the great room.

For the kitchen design, it took a long time for us to decide exactly what to do. Even though this is a task-oriented space, we still wanted it to be a unique and vibrant room. In the beginning, we just weren't sure exactly how to get there. We painted and repainted it, then settled on black cabinets and an oriental rug, not only to make a strong visual statement but to provide balance with the wood walls. The dramatic dark cabinets, and the black and red in the rug reflect the richness of the blond wood perfectly.

When we first took the leap and painted the cabinets black, we were concerned that the dark tone would be depressing and make it difficult to work in the room. It turned out to be a restful color and our task lighting makes food prep very easy and relaxing—which was the point of building a log cabin in the first place. The bold kitchen décor also blends with the strong design tone of the rest of the cabin. It took a while, but we're finally happy with the outcome.

At first, the kitchen didn't even have a window, but then we added on a dining room adjacent to it that is almost all glass. The result is that we now have this cloistered kitchen space that still has all the light and air we would want from the outside. It all works just right in our cabin home. ¤

BATHROOMS

I t would appear that all of us who are more than two years old know what a bathroom is for—or do we? Because cabin living can redefine our lifestyle, we should look at how each of its spaces, including the bathrooms, contributes to the optimum form and function of the rest of the cabin. With innovative design, cabin bathrooms solve several practical needs for the entire home while potentially offering a truly spa-like romantic ambiance.

WHAT TO INCORPORATE

Those fortunate enough to have a piece of land with a great view on which their cabin is sited should usually put at least one window in the bathroom. The best use of the window might be alongside a bathtub so that when soaking in bubbles, a great view is part of the bathing experience. Some other practical ideas:

- ☞ Enclosed commode area
- ☞ Linen & towel closet
- ☞ Book and magazine rack
- ☞ Separate tub and shower area

This sink was cleverly created in a guest bedroom.

Facing:
This is definitely not Grandpa's outhouse. The warm apple green walls and pine tub surround create a comfortable, colorful country ambiance.

Each of these elements makes the most use of the bathroom, especially in the master bathroom, where the room is likely to be a shared space.

Following are a couple of "outside of the box" ideas. Because part of the cabin experience is to be able to relax and conserve energy and steps, the bathroom can become the ideal space to include other activities you wouldn't normally consider:

☛ Do laundry and iron: Since the kitchen is often open to the rest of the great room, unless you have a separate laundry room, putting the washer and dryer in the kitchen is unsightly. On the other hand, placing laundry facilities either adjacent to the bathroom or behind louvered doors in the bathroom itself is ideal. Considering that one gets undressed to shower in the bathroom and dirty towels stem from that room as well, it makes sense to put laundry facilities nearby.

☛ Think of your bathroom as a home gym: Workout equipment, high on function and low on ambiance, is decidedly unappealing in the middle of the great room or the bedroom. However, it is practical and convenient to stow it in a bathroom nook, out of sight and within jump-in distance of the shower. You can really go for the burn in style!

☛ Take time to smell the roses: Install an overhead-mounted television and/or built-in speaker system. Even without workout equipment, the bathroom makes a nice extra haven in which to bathe while enjoying music. Think of your bathroom as not just a place for necessities but as a private little getaway within your getaway.

(continued p. 135)

Contemporary water-jet relaxation is not incongruous in this old-fashioned, woodsy space.

Facing:
This bathroom is customized for a good view while enjoying a bubbled soak.

Facing:
This older cabin has a practical shower enclosure with a unique towel rack.

A partial glass block wall is a great system for baths—it provides light while also allowing for privacy without chopping up a space into claustrophobic compartments.

Southwest design is featured in this innovative bath, a continuation of which is shown above.

A BATHROOM FOR NOW AND LATER

BY TOMMI JAMISON ☞ PROJECT DESIGNER AND MARKETING MANAGER, HEARTHSTONE, INC., DANDRIDGE, TENNESSEE

When building a bathroom, don't think in terms of retrofitting down the line. It is far less expensive to give some thought at the outset on what you want now and what you might need later. It is much easier to plan ahead for the just-in-cases than it is to remodel an environment as our needs change.

Whether your cabin is a full-time home or vacation getaway, bathroom musts include at least one full bath on the main floor. This includes a sink, water closet (toilet) and shower or tub/shower combo. If a master suite is located on the first and main floor, consider an additional one-half bath or powder room that can be used by guests. The master bath is such a personal and private place; it can be a more relaxed environment if only the homeowners utilize it.

Although women are known for wanting luxurious bubble baths and men are expected to live for long, hot showers, neither of these stereotypes is necessarily true. And who says we can't have both? More and more cabin bathrooms now feature a separate tub and shower.

In all cabin rooms, including the bathrooms, another simple and inexpensive must-have is 3-foot-wide interior doors. Although exterior doors are at least the standard 3 feet wide, it is less common but highly practical to have the same for interior doors instead of the standard 2 feet 8 inches. Then if the unforeseen happens and a wheelchair becomes either a temporary or a permanent fixture, it is much easier to maneuver through 3-foot-wide doors than 2-foot 8-inch openings. Quite often 2-foot 8-inch doors must be removed from the hinges to accommodate a wheelchair.

The bathroom should also be user-friendly for all generations; we all get older (or hope we do). Consider having plenty of floor space for turnaround access (The Americans with Disabilities Act requires 5 feet of minimum floor space for turnaround). Once again, think about wheelchairs, walkers or multiple users for additional assistance. If finances permit, a wonderful feature is to include a walk-in/wheel-in shower. This feature can also add resale value. Another good reason for extra floor space in the master bath is that it is often used by more than one person at a time. One in the shower, one at the sink—everyone needs some turn-around space.

You should also consider these sound technical tips:

☞ When designing the floor plan of your custom dream bath, an essential consideration is the amount of floor area that is required to accommodate and comfortably use the fixtures. The term "fixtures" refers to the lavatory (or sink), water closet, and bathtub and/or shower. The floor area required from the front edge of a lavatory to the opposite wall or other obstruction is 18 inches for the activity

(continued p. 128)

Many homeowners find it very practical to have a separate tub area.

Keeping it simple and old-fashioned is perfect in a weekend getaway cabin. Note that the hand-painted design on the bathtub repeats the motif of the wallpaper pattern.

zone. This is where the user will stand to wash hands, etc., plus an additional 30 inches for a circulation zone. Therefore, the total floor space required is, at a minimum, 48 square inches, or 4 square feet.

☞ When designing a separate water closet, the requirements are slightly different. Here, a circulation zone usually isn't required, because the water closet is usually located at the end of the room, or in a separate room to itself. Under these circumstances, the necessary size or depth of the water closet sometimes varies. A good rule to follow is that there should be a minimum of 24 inches for the activity zone; once again, this is from the front edge of the water closet to the opposite wall or other obstruction. For the width of the water closet, there should be a minimum of 3 feet. This means that from the center of the water closet to the wall or any other obstruction, there should be a minimum of 18 inches to the left and 18 inches to the right.

☞ There should be a minimum of 30 inches of floor area in front of a bathtub/shower and it is preferred that a 36-inch minimum is used. Of course, these are not handicap-accessible criteria. Someone in a wheelchair could maneuver in these spaces, but it would be hard and awkward. So, it is highly recommended to allow more than just these minimums.

☞ Another bath element to consider is what glass to use where. Tub and shower windows must be of tempered glass (in case of a fall). It is recommended that bathroom windows to the exterior be wider than tall and fairly high off the floor. Consider that what you want is plenty of light in the room while maintaining privacy. ▢

Facing:
In designing a bathroom, remember that it is a place where you can be funky, have fun and enjoy your sense of humor.

Ample space is left around this tub and sink/vanity area to maneuver through the morning routine.

This bathroom, in a wooded environment,
is a getaway within a getaway.

Facing:
Fanciful romance is the design theme
in this cabin bath.

This practical space divider creates a bathroom that can be used by more than one person at a time. Vintage furnishings and collectibles meld gently with the log walls.

Facing:
Architectural design plays the starring
role in this cabin bathroom. It's about as
rustic as you can get and still be indoors.

This bath promotes the simple
rustic pleasures. Notice the use of
bark trim on the vanity and twig
handle on the vanity door.

Facing:
Expansive space is highlighted by a great
mountain view offering the all-time dilemma:
do you look in the mirror or out the window?

HOW MANY, HOW BIG?

When people lived in early cabins, a bathroom meant a separate outdoor facility. These hearty souls entertained the hope that the winter winds would not blow it over—especially when occupied. Now, thankfully, when we design cabins, we consider just how many bathrooms we need and how large they should be—and they're all inside.

Unless you are building a cabin for one or two people, and at the notion of visitors you lock the doors and turn off the lights and hide, more than one bathroom is essential. In fact, most cabin keepers welcome guests, albeit for short periods. Considering

this, the recommendation by room designers and anyone who has ever had company is to install a bathroom directly off the front entranceway within easy access of the great room. This can be either a full bath (meaning the inclusion of shower and/or tub) or a half-bath (just the basics: toilet and sink).

Generally, the master bathroom is the largest and most fully appointed. However, within financial feasibility and space allowances, one should consider one bathroom per guest room or at least a half bath—sink and commode. This ensures happier guests and more privacy for everyone.

(continued p. 144)

Facing:
Design contrasts add a unique look in log baths. The crystal chandelier is eye-catching and unexpected and adds an accent of sophistication.

Although compact, this guest bath contains all the necessities.

A small space is well designed and utilized by matching the tub surround to the log walls.

Facing:
An old-time tub, wash-bowl and pitcher on an Empire-style chest give this new cabin bathroom a vintage look. The corresponding style of a free-standing pedestal sink is readily available from major manufacturers.

An antique door and built-in collection nook create unique old-world ambiance.

It's in the smallest details: tile countertops and western-themed textiles on the bench create a Southwestern mood in this new log cabin.

Facing:
A simple, low-set border adds individuality
without overwhelming this small bath.

Simplicity reigns—claw-foot tub, good art
and one great rug have design impact
while not cluttering the look.

A well-placed window lets the sun pour onto logs; it's the only design statement this bath needs.

Facing:
Wood outside and in, this cabin bathroom has all the basics. It's a comfortable space without frills.

Gingham window treatments add an accent of color.

Antique-style cabinet hinges and a few collectibles make a quiet design statement. The rounded window and mirror emphasize the flowing nature of the rough log siding and beams.

RUSTIC RETREAT OR CONTEMPORARY SPA

As for design, bathrooms generally match the architecture of the rest of the cabin. If the rest of the cabin is Adirondack in style, deep woody tones and twig furnishings can be carried over here. If the cabin décor is English cottage, then any interior walls can be drywalled and painted in pastels and accented with floral towels. And if the rest of the house is done in early cowboy, boots and lassoes can be hung from almost anything.

Back-to-basics simplicity and skilled craftsmanship are the keys to Arts & Crafts style. Here, homeowners have carried that theme from the architecture to bathroom design.

*Facing:
Contemporary Americana collectibles add a delightful dimension to this log bathroom.*

A simple, Early American–style lighting fixture adds elegance to this bath. Note the apple ladder towel rack viewed in the mirror.

Don't forget that the bathroom is still a room to be enjoyed. By all means, hang artwork and display collections. The only potential drawback is that some objects react negatively to steam and dampness if you don't have proper ventilation or if they're too close to the shower. Other than that, sculpture, paintings and all the rest of your favorite things belong here as much as in any other place in the cabin.

One good-sized design piece speaks volumes in a small bath.

Bathrooms are as good a place as any for unique art. In this case, the design flourishes were handmade by the homeowner.

Décor is kept to a minimum while the log structure and the view are highlighted; anything additional might have been overkill.

Facing:
Wallpaper changes the mood of this bathroom from conservative to fun.

Corporate America certainly recognizes that cabin owners want their bathrooms to be as attractive as the rest of the house. To that end, many companies manufacturing bathroom fixtures and appliances make products designed to fit especially well within the design aesthetic of cabins. For example, Kohler now offers one toilet painted with scenes of Montana fly-fishing and another with yacht racing. Both capture the ambiance of outdoor activities associated with cabin living.

(continued p. 159)

Just a couple of brightly colored and patterned towels can add a lot to a simple bath.

Facing:
Homeowners clearly had fun shopping for the southwestern-themed details of their unusual cabin bath. Items such as these are either manufactured or made by talented artisans.

LOOKING GOOD

BY JUDY BRACHT ☞ BATHROOM DESIGNER, STUART KITCHENS, McLEAN, VIRGINIA

When it comes to cabin bathroom design, my immediate response is to focus on elements of nature (natural as opposed to man-made materials) and a handcrafted look. I opt for wood cabinetry and trim of either cherry, for its red tones, or maple or oak because their lighter golden tones blend well with logs. Dark, rich finishes also work well. Among the most popular tone now is a shade called "balsamic" (a very deep brown). To further enhance a rustic design, door and window moldings should be slightly wider than in a more contemporary room.

Keep in mind the following tips:

☞ When possible, countertops should be thicker than the standard 1½ inches. Counters up to 3 inches thick are really striking.

☞ Think in terms of utilizing natural counter materials of wood, slate, soapstone or honed granite, which also blend well with log and wood walls.

☞ When designing a cabin bath, consider using a mixture of antique-style freestanding furniture with hand pegging and matte finishes juxtaposed against premade bathroom vanities.

☞ Ideally, fittings, faucets and other hardware are of brushed nickel or oiled brass in a matte finish.

☞ Arts & Crafts design works well in cabins and this carries into the bath. The muted, natural, monochromatic color palette, clean architectural lines and ceramic tiles with images of natural elements such as bugs and leaves in relief bring in high style without jarring the senses. This works particularly well with log and other wood and rustic surrounds. ¤

Facing:
The cabinetry matches, but the homeowner's design accents create a personalized look. Ceiling height adds a sense of spaciousness.

A freestanding towel rack gives individuality to this spacious cabin bathroom.

Facing:
In this bath, the woodsy-themed cabinetry creates the entire look. Note the light switch and the exaggerated cabinet door pulls.

Just a little stenciling in the corner provides an interesting design touch and an old-world look.

An age-old great combo: pine and plaid.
The shower curtain, in its bold pattern,
is perfect with wood and log walls.

Facing:
Homeowners took advantage of multiple windows
and a luscious view in placing their large tub.

Another terrific textural blend is wood and glass. Above, a simple glass shelf and a super-sized mirror create the dressing room portion of the bathroom.

Facing:
Matching colors in the bedroom and bath make the entire space appealing and inviting.

ENJOYING THE PROCESS
AS WELL AS THE PRODUCT

Based on the theory that the master bathroom is a space that will be visited by fewer cabin guests than other rooms, and that the cabin is a great place to try out design notions from the recesses of your imagination, this is a perfect place to take some innovative decorative chances. Depending on your plumbing and carpentry skills, and your patience-to-frustration ratio, you could take on some of these projects yourself.

☞ New thinking about sinks: Consider a sink sunk into a barrel or antique dresser. Or you could forget about the sink surround altogether and mount a wonderfully decorated bowl, drilled out for a drain, placed on the wall for a one-of-a-kind bathroom element. Faucets can then be set into the wall above it.

☞ For storage: Hang shelves and trim them in anything from fringe to lace. They make just as good storage for towels and supplies set in baskets as any bathroom-specific manufactured products.

☞ Floor it: Almost nothing installed in a house or cabin is inexpensive. The floor can be at the top of the list for costly building elements if you consider ceramic tile, stone or hardwood. One suggestion is to put down plywood and paint or stain it in anything from stenciled plaid or faux marble to big, bold checks. Just one solid color is great too. Then give it at least four coats of sealer. When done properly, your floor will be of your own design at a fraction of the cost of other natural or manufactured flooring products. ¤

These painted sinks guarantee a one-of-a-kind look to the bathroom. If you can't find ones you like, buy plain white and go to town with porcelain paint. Check with your paint store before you undertake this venture; they can offer technical advice. Note the family picture gallery viewed in the mirror.

Facing:
This log archway makes a grand entrance to a diminutive area. Notice how the skylight adds light and needed space. When combined with careful planning, free-rein creativity pays off.

Facing:
Just a few individual touches make this Southwestern–style bath uniquely tailored to the homeowner's personality: a miniature Harley on display, stainedglass window and potted cactus.

Necessity is the mother of invention. This is one of the smallest baths we've seen, but it beats walking downstairs in the middle of the night.

RESOURCES

PHOTOGRAPHERS

Franklin & Esther Schmidt
F & E Schmidt Photography
feschmidt@earthlink.net
www.FESchmidtPhotography.com

LOG & TIMBER FRAME MAGAZINES & SHOW PRODUCERS

Country's Best Log Homes Magazine
Luxury Log Homes & Timberframe Magazine
PO Box 1643
Williamsport, PA 17703
800.219.1187

Country's Best Log & Timber Home Show
(Twice a year in various parts of the country)
800.210.1187
www.countrysbestloghomesmag.com

Log Home Design Ideas Magazine
1620 South Lawe Street, Suite 2
Appleton, WI 54915
800.573.1900
www.LHDI.com

Log Home Living Magazine
Timber Frame Homes Magazine
Home Buyer Publications, Inc.
4125 Lafayette Center Drive, Suite 100
Chantilly, VA 20151
800.826.3893
www.Loghomeliving.com

Log Home Living Home Shows
(Offered periodically throughout the year)
800.782.1253
www.loghomeliving.com

Log Homes Illustrated Magazine
www.loghomesmag.com

Timber Homes Illustrated Magazine
www.mcmillencomm.com

Log Home & Timber Frame Expo
(Throughout the country: January through May; September through January)
888.LOG.EXPO (564.3976)
www.logexpo.com

LOG & TIMBER HOME BUILDERS

Anthony Log Homes
2224 Brevard Road
Arden, NC 28704
800.837.8786
www.anthonyloghomes.com

Appalachian Log Homes, Inc.
11312 Station West Drive
Knoxville, TN 37922
800.726.0708
www.alhloghomes.com

Appalachian Log Structures
PO Box 614
Ripley, WV 25271
800.458.9990
www.applog.com

Bullock and Company
PO Box 44 New Lowell
Ontario, Canada LOM 1NO
705.424.5222
www.bullockloghomes.com

Caribou Creek Log Homes
HCR, Box 3
Bonners Ferry, ID 83805
800.619.1156
www.cariboucreekloghomes.com

Cornerstone Log & Timber Homes, LLC
1854-A Hendersonville Road
Box 208
Asheville, NC 28803
800.255.4713
www.cornerstoneloghomes.com

Country Log Homes
79 Clayton Road
Ashley Falls, MA
413.229.8084
www.countryloghomes.com

Fireside Log Homes
516 River Street
PO Box 1136
Ellijay, GA 30540
800.521.LOGS (5647)
www.firesideloghomes.com

Hearthstone, Inc.
1630 East Highway 25/70
Dandridge, TN 37725
800. 247.4442
www.hearthstonehomes.com

Hilltop Log Homes
88 Pond Road
PO Box 170
Bowdoinham, ME 04008
800.622.4608

Honest Abe Log Homes
3855 Clay County Highway
Moss, TN 38575
800.231.3695
www.honestabe.com

Jim Barna Log Systems
22459 Alberta Street
Oneida, TN 37841
800.962.4734
www.logcabins.com

Kuhns Bros Log Homes, Inc.
390 Swarz Road
Lewisburg, PA 17837
800.326.9614
www.kuhnsbros.com

Log Homes of America, Inc.
9649-1 Hwy 105 South
Banner Elk, NC 28604
800.564.8496
www.loghomesofamerica.com

Montana Log Homes
3250 Highway 93 South
Kalispel, MT 59901
www.montanaloghomes.com

Northeastern Log Homes, Inc.
PO Box 126
Groton, VT 05046
800.992.6526
www.northeasternlog.com

Real Log Homes
PO Box 202
Hartland, VT 05048
802.436.2130
www.realloghomes.com

Southland Log Homes, Inc.
7521 Broad River Road
PO Box 1668
Irmo, SC 29063
888.883.8884
www.southlandloghomes.com

StoneMill Log Homes
10024 Parkside Drive
Knoxville, TN 37922
800.438.8274
www.stonemill.com

Tennessee Log Homes
2537 Decatur Pike
Athens, TN 37303
800.251.9218
www.tnloghomes.com

Timberpeg
800.636.2424
www.timberpeg.com

Ward Log Homes
39 Bangor Street
PO Box 72
Houlton, ME
800.341.1566
www.wardloghomes.com

Wilderness Log Homes
PO Box 902
Plymouth, WI 53073
800.558.5812
www.thewildernesscompany.com

Yankee Barn Homes
131 Yankee Barn Road
Grantham, NH 03753
800.258.9786
www.yankeebarnhomes.com

ONLINE LOG RESOURCE

Gina Batchelor
Log Home Solutions
3647 Sunset Avenue, Box 331
Rocky Mount, NC 27804
866.451.9984
www.loghomesolutions.com

WINDOWS & DOORS

Andersen Corporation
100 Fourth Avenue North
Bayport, MN 55003
651.264.5150
www.andersenwindows.com

Kolbe & Kolbe
1323 South 11th Avenue
Wausau, WI 54401
800.955.8177
www.kolbe-kolbe.com

Marvin Windows and Doors
PO Box 100
Warroad, MN 56763
888.537.7828
www.marvin.com

Velux (skylights)
800.88.VELUX (800.888.3589)
www.velux.com

KITCHEN & BATHROOM PLUMBING APPLIANCES AND FIXTURES

Jacuzzi
2121 North California Boulevard
Walnut Creek, CA 94596
800.288.4002
www.jacuzzi.com

Kohler
444 Highland Drive
Kohler, WI 53044
800.456.4537
www.kohler.com

Waterworks
800.927.2120
www.waterworks.com

LARGE APPLIANCE INFORMATION

ONLINE INFORMATION RESOURCES SPECIALIZING IN VINTAGE-STYLE APPLIANCES
www.appliance411.com

ANTIQUE APPLIANCE RESTORATIONS
AntiqueAppliances.com
30 West Savannah Street
PO Box 389
Clayton, GA 30525
706.782.7326
www.antiqueappliances.com

CABINETMAKERS

Mill's Pride
2 Easton Oval
Columbus, OH 43219
800.441.0337
www.millspride.com

Plain & Fancy Custom Cabinetry
800.447.9006
www.plainfancycabinetry.com

Wood-Mode Inc.
1 - 2nd Street
Kreamer, PA 17833
877.635.7500
www.wood-mode.com

INFORMATIONAL RESOURCE ON CABINETS
Kitchen Cabinet Manufacturers Association
1899 Preston White Drive
Reston, VA 20191
703.264.1690
www.kcma.org

FIREPLACES & STOVES

Vermont Castings
Majestic Fireplaces
410 Admiral Boulevard
Mississauga, Ontario, Canada L5T 2N6
905.670.7777
www.myownfireplace.com

DESIGNERS

ART & ANTIQUES

Avram Finklestein and Phil Montana
Gold Goat
6119 Route 9
Rhinebeck, NY 12572
845.876.1582
www.goldgoat.com

INTERIORS

Michael Buchanan Style
245 - 7th Avenue
New York, NY 10001
michaelbuchananstyle@yahoo.com

KITCHENS

Harriet Finder, CKD
Stuart Kitchens
1359 Beverly Road
McLean, VA 22101
703.734.6102
www.stuartkitchens.com

Heather Chong
HMChong@aol.com

BATHROOMS

Judith Bracht
Stuart Kitchens
1359 Beverly Road
McLean, VA 22101
703.734.6102
www.stuartkitchens.com

TEXTILES

Waverly
800.423.5881
www.waverly.com

RUGS

Claire Murray
PO Box 390
Ascutney, VT 05030
800.252.4733
www.clairemurray.com

FLOORING AND CEILINGS

Flooring Guide
www.flooringguide.com

Armstrong World Industries
2500 Columbia Avenue
PO Box 3001
Lancaster, PA 17604
800.233.3823
www.armstrong.com

KITCHENWARE & FURNISHINGS

Le Creuset
877.273.8738
www.lecreuset.com

Plow and Hearth
800.494.7544
www.plowhearth.com

NOTE: SOME IMAGES FOR THIS BOOK
WERE PHOTOGRAPHED AT
Inn at Maple Crossing
RR1, Box 129, Maple Lake
Mentor, MN 56736
218.637.6600
www.innatmaplecrossing.com